James Martin Peebles

Spiritual Harmonies

James Martin Peebles

Spiritual Harmonies

ISBN/EAN: 9783337334680

Printed in Europe, USA, Canada, Australia, Japan

Cover: Foto ©Lupo / pixelio.de

More available books at **www.hansebooks.com**

SPIRITUAL HARMONIES,

OR

SPIRITUAL TEACHINGS,

Songs and Hymns.

WITH

APPROPRIATE READINGS FOR FUNERALS.

By J. M. PEEBLES, M. D.

I heard the voice of harpers harping with their harps.
And they sung as it were a new song.

SECOND EDITION.

BOSTON:
COLBY AND RICH, PUBLISHERS,
No. 9 Montgomery Place.
1880.

COPYRIGHT,
1880,
BY J. M. PEEBLES.

Stereotyped at the Boston Stereotype Foundry,
No. 4 Pearl Street.

PREFACE.

"The Spiritual Songster and Teacher" having been so favorably received by the public, — six large editions having been sold, — I deem it practical to remodel, improve, and greatly enlarge it, adding songs new and old, with original and selected readings for funeral occasions; so that, for a trifle of expense, our friends may have, for seances, Sunday gatherings, and camp-meetings, a general statement of the belief of Spiritualists, responsive readings, songs, hymns, and words of comfort for seasons of sickness and death.

It will be conceded that old music and old songs that are really good and rich in melody are infinitely preferable to new ones too poor and too common to stir the soul's depths or kindle the fires of inspiration.

In defining Spiritualism, I define it only for myself; and yet, in all probability, I reflect the general opinions of the millions in America known as Spiritualists.

I am confident that the religious element has failed

to receive sufficient attention among us. But now — if I rightly read the signs of the times — there is a growing desire in our ranks to promote order, culture, stability, religious enthusiasm, and the Christ-spirit of truth, purity, and harmony; and singing — especially congregational singing — is a potent help to this end.

J. M. PEEBLES.

SPIRITUALISM,

AND ITS GENERAL TEACHINGS.

Man, a thinking, reasoning, and morally responsible being, is the crowning glory of God. He is furthermore a trinity in structure, made up of the soul, of a spiritual and of an earthly body.

The soul, the conscious innermost of man, is a potentialized portion of the deific life, incarnated in the material body for a more potent individualization, and for necessary experiences in the realm of matter.

Death, just as natural in a ripe old age as birth, is the severing of the copartnership existing between the spiritual and the earthly body.

Man is naturally a religious being, and the seals of his manhood are consciousness and intuition, reason and aspiration. And further, man desires to live again; desires to meet his friends in the higher life; desires to know and love them, and with them progress through eternity. And right here comes in Spiritualism, with its facts, its tangible proofs, and its *positive knowledge* of a future existence. But

WHAT IS SPIRITUALISM?

Defined in general terms, it implies — *the possibility and certainty of a present conscious intercourse with the inhabitants of the spirit-world.* "Are they not all ministering spirits?" asked the apostle.

In a broader sense, Spiritualism is a phenomenon, a philosophy, and a religion; appealing to the sensuous perceptions through the manifestations and materializations of mediumship; to the reason through a calm, cultured judgment, and to the soul's religious affections through and by inspiring spiritual growth and purity of life. It is not new in the world. The records of India and Egypt—the Old and the New Testaments abound in descriptions of angel appearings and spiritual manifestations; in prevision dream and trance; in oracles, prophecies, levitations, visions, healing gifts; and, to use the apostle's language, "the discerning of spirits." Genuine spiritual manifestations, therefore, are not only in perfect accord with the marvels of the New Testament; but they are the "greater works" promised by Jesus Christ to believers—the living witnesses of immortality.

SPIRITUALISTS, THEREFORE,

Believe in the Infinite Presence, the Divine Energy, one living and true God, wisdom and love. And upon the pulsing bosom of this God is the soul's rest forever.

Believe in Jesus, accepting Peter's definition, "Jesus of Nazareth, a *man* approved of God among you by miracles, wonders, and signs." (Acts ii. 22.) Other New Testament writers denominate him the "Son of Joseph," our "Elder Brother," who went about doing good.

Believe in the Holy Spirit as a refined, etherealized aural substance that like forked flames "sat upon the disciples"—that "fell upon those who heard Peter," and was "poured out upon the Gentiles." All those who have been touched by the purifying influences of the Christ-principle, may impart this holy spiritual substance by "the laying on of hands."

Believe in Inspiration, a spiritual infilling from the Divine Fountain from ministering angels, and from the beautiful in nature. Prophets and apostles, martyrs and reformers, were inspired in the past and are in the present.

Believe in Repentance as implying sorrow for wrongdoing, and reformation. But in no way does it promise escape from the legitimate consequences of violated law. Nature holding the golden scales of justice says obey and enjoy--transgress and suffer.

Believe in Rewards and Punishments, as links in the chain of cause and effect. Retribution is inevitable. In all worlds man as a spiritual being is a moral actor, a subject of law, and responsible—reaping anguish from vice, and happiness from virtue. Memory, the backward looking eye of the soul, accompanies each individual to the world of spirits—that House of "Many Mansions." Each when leaving the mortal body gravitates by virtue of fixed law to his appropriate zone or spiritual plane of existence. The purer and more Christ-like the life on earth, the more ecstatic will be the bliss in that beautiful homeland of the angels.

Divine love reaches down to the lowest sphere. Progress spans all worlds. Angels are ever inviting those in the lower spheres to "come up higher." Every sweet thought breathed, every generous word uttered, every charitable deed wrought, and every heart-beat for virtue, purity, and peace, will live forever—live to beautify and bless!

Spiritualism settles three questions of momentous import:

I. That man has a conscious existence beyond the grave.

II. That all individuals commence that existence precisely as they leave this, mentally and morally, retaining their identity and memory.

III. That this future existence is one of mental progress and spiritual unfoldment for all human intelligences.

The spiritual philosophy, while undermining the false and overthrowing the Babels of bigotry and superstition, is constructive in purpose, and eclectic in method. It gladly conserves the good and adopts the right and true wherever found.

Spiritualism, as interpreted by its best exponents, has

given free thought a new impetus. It has severed the bonds of fear and superstition, revealed in a truer light the law of compensation, opened to anxious eyes a revised geography of the heavens, and convinced multitudes of atheists and deists of a future conscious existence. Unbarring the gates of death, it has brought the loved inhabitants of the summer-land into our cities, our homes, our chambers, permitting us to touch their shining hands and listen to the music of their voices.

It has encouraged the desponding, comforted the sick, and with the tender hand of sympathy brushed away the mourner's tears.

The apostle Paul's injunction was, "Add to your faith, knowledge." Spiritualists, studying the manifestations, have done this. While showing the naturalness of converse with the spirit-world by sympathy, vision, trance, impressions, and inspirations, the tendency of Spiritualism is to elevate the thoughts, encourage fidelity, spiritualize the affections, induce true righteousness, and promote the principles of fraternity and equality. Underlying all reform movements, physiological and social, philanthropic and religious, it would strike the "axe at the root of the tree," by rightly generating, then wisely educating, all the nations of the earth. As a moral power, it is eminently apostolic. Its invocations are soul-felt aspirations.

Kindling in believing souls the loftiest endeavor, the broadest tolerance, the noblest charity, and the warmest heart-fellowship; its prayers are good deeds; its music the sweet breathings of guardian angels; its ideal, the Christ-life of perfection, and its temple the measureless universe of God.

Oh, come let us worship in this holy temple!

READINGS AND RESPONSES.

LESSON I.

Ministering angels of purity, peace, and love are with us. Oh, come let us worship
In spirit and in truth.
All true aspiration, all noble effort is worship.

Nature continually calls with many voices to worship in her temple—a temple consecrated to the good of humanity.

Infinite Presence—Our Father and Mother, wisdom and love—help; O heavenly intelligences! help us to love the good, the pure, and the true.

And help us further to practice the divine principles that we profess.

Lead us onward, O divine Wisdom!

Lead us into green pastures and by the side of still waters, O evangels of truth.

These signs shall follow them that believe:

They shall heal the sick and cast out demons.

And, behold, the lame shall walk, the blind shall see, the deaf shall hear, and the dumb shall sing for joy.

And all because the " spirit of truth is come"— the ministry of angels.

LESSON II.

Angels stand by the pure in heart in their transfigured beauty, and surround them with a sphere of light and love.

They come to lead weary pilgrims from the rude scenes of life to the mansions of rest.

They make life's barren wastes to bloom like the gardens of paradise.

Their presence throws around us a holy calm.

Pure love is the soul's divine magnet. Love one heart truly and you love all; for all souls are but streams flowing from the great central Soul of the universe.

God is love—and we are members one of another.

If thy brother shall trespass against thee, go and tell him his fault between thee and him alone.

Forgive unto seventy times seven.

Be not forgetful to entertain strangers; for thereby some have entertained angels unawares.

Every good act is charity.

Putting a wanderer in the right way—removing stones and thorns from the road is charity.

Faith, hope, charity—these three; but the greatest of these is charity.

Write over the portals of your inmost souls, Sacred to purity.

Then will the angels abide with us.

LESSON III.

The sunshine of the heart is revealed in the smile, the glance, the musical speech, and the aura of goodness that encircles those who truly love their kind.

All humanity constitutes the family of God.

The Divine Spirit breathes into us the breath of life—and accordingly, we bear the Divine image.

We are all painters and sculptors. We "grow to be like what we feed upon."

Every spirit builds itself a house, and beyond its house a world, and beyond its world a heaven.

Even our bodies should be fit temples for holy spirits to dwell in.

The universal human heart, though blind and cold and sefish, pays homage to purity.

"The pure in heart," said Jesus, "shall see God."

Purity, peace, and "all things in common"—these are the foundation stones in the Temple of truth—the Christ-church that shall usher in the millennial morn of the nations.

Then shall the wolf dwell with the lamb, and the leopard shall lie down with the kid, ... and a little child shall lead them.

Revenge and cruelty are among the vices of cowards.

To err is human:—and to forgive and forget the errors and wrongs of others is divine.

LESSON IV.

Human life is comparable to a journey—a pilgrimage to the better land.

We shall know each other there.

There are green meadows in the spirit-land; there are deep, mossy banks; there are clear meandering streams; there are stars of diamond beauty; there are harps of coral gems; there are schools and lyceums; fields and fountains, gardens and massive libraries—*everything* to charm, educate, and unfold the soul.

I heard a voice from the angel-world, saying, Come up higher.

Prophets and apostles, martyrs and reformers continue there holy missions in the land of souls.

Spirit life is an active life; a social life; a retributive life; a constructive life; and a progressive life. Reason and affection, conscience and memory go with us into the future state of existence.

"Are they not all ministering spirits?"

The heart softens at the sound of angel footsteps within our homes.

Why come the angels to our earth?

They come to demonstrate a future conscious existence; to guide our feet in the paths of virtue and wisdom; to comfort all that mourn, and lead us into the green pastures of purity and peace.

The light of their love is the sunshine of our souls. They call upon us to overcome the world—to create the heaven now that we hope to enjoy hereafter.

It doth not yet appear what we shall be.

LESSON V.

Calmness and quietness with a conscious self-balance—*these* constitute the golden mean in social life.

Be not disturbed because of evil-doers. Vices bring their own compensations.

The way of the transgressor is hard.

Great peace have those who obey the physical, mental, and moral laws of their being.

To affirm thyself, to preserve thyself, to celebrate thyself, to harmonize thyself, to trust thyself, and to redeem thyself—making use of all true aids—*these* are among the maxims of the age.

We will be free in thought, aspirational in purpose, and harmonial in life.

There is a higher law—a law written by the finger of God upon the tablets of the human soul.

That heart cannot be true to others, which is false to itself.

Truth and sincerity, integrity and justice—these are the foundation stones in the true character.

As the fruition of faith is knowledge; so the result of good works is heaven—a present heaven on earth.

LESSON VI.

How sweet and perfect is the child's faith in the parent, and how firm should be ours in the Divine goodness of God, and the innate goodness of man! Under the ice the water runs; above the clouds the sun shines; upon the mouldering piles of India, and the marbled ruins of Greece, mosses are green, and wild vines climb sunward. So, nestling under the roughest exterior, and growing out from every conscious soul, there is something fair and beautiful.

Each and all have their angel sides.

Life and death are both beautiful links in the chain of endless being.

The ministry of angels and spirits verifies the promise of Jesus—" These signs shall follow them that believe."

Beloved, believe not every spirit, but try the spirits whether they are of God; because many false prophets are gone out into the world.

The spiritual philosophy, spanning science, morality and pure religion, is God's living word to humanity.

He that hath an ear, let him hear what the Spirit saith unto the churches.

Blessed is the man that endureth temptation: for when he is tried, he shall receive the crown of life.

He that hath an ear, let him hear what the Spirit saith unto the churches.

After this I looked, and behold, a door was opened in heaven: and I heard as it were a trumpet talking with me; which said, Come up hither, and I will show thee things which must be hereafter.

He that hath an ear, let him hear what the Spirit saith unto the churches.

He that overcometh the same shall be clothed in white raiment: and I will not blot his name out of the book of life, ... and he shall eat of the hidden manna, and I will give him a white stone, and in the stone a new name written, which no man knoweth save he that receiveth it. And I will give him the morning star.

LESSON VII.

What is truth? Truth is the soul's deepest and divinest conviction. Our conceptions of truth unfold as the soul expands and approaches the more perfect standard, the absolute. "Sanctify them through the truth," was the prayer of Jesus.

Ye shall know the truth, and the truth shall make you free.

Let Truth and Falsehood grapple; who ever knew Truth put to the worst in a fair and open encounter?

Obey God as manifest in thine own soul.

Human life is a struggle. Good and evil meet and commingle upon the earth as upon an arena for battle.

Be not alarmed—fear not.

Good shall be triumphant, and vanquish her opposing armies.

The terror of the conflict shall pass away as the cloud passeth, and sunshine and peace shall succeed it.

Quietness shall rest upon our valleys, and glory upon our mountains.

Righteousness shall flow in our streets like a river, and human hearts shall be the temples where angels dwell.

Dawn breaks through rosy billows of clouds, and glides on into a broader blaze of glory.

The future is full of promise.

Every winter hath its spring, every ocean its shining gems, every frost its shining crystals, and every thunder-storm its compensating atmosphere of purity.

Every cloud hath its silver lining, every ruin its growing vines, every wave-tossed ark its dove, every blood-stained cross its flower-wreathed crown; and for every paradise lost, there are thousands to be gained.

"Give ear," said the old Aryan of India, "to the instructions of prudence, and let the precepts of truth sink deep into your hearts, O my children! So shall the charms of your minds add lustre to the elegance of your forms; and your beauty, like the rose it resembles, shall retain its sweetness when the bloom is withered."

Absolute purity of heart and life is the richest human possession.

LESSON VIII.

What is man? a thinking, reasoning, spiritual being, constituted of a physical body, a spiritual body, and the soul, which soul is a portion of the Divine Soul—God incarnate.

The soul sustains a similar relation to God that does the stream to the living fountain.

Death is a ripple upon the ocean of existence; a shedding of the physical body; a birth into the better-land—up one step higher.

Life and death in the economy of nature are as natural as they are beautiful.

There's a land far away 'mid the stars, we are told,
  Where they know not the sorrows of time;
Where the pure waters wander through valleys of
    gold,
  And life is a treasure sublime.
. . . .
Oh! the stars never tread the blue heavens at night,
  But we think where the ransomed have trod;
And the Day never smiles from his palace of light,
  But we feel the bright smile of our God.
We are travelling homeward through changes and
    gloom
  To a kingdom where pleasures unceasingly bloom,
And our Guide is the glory that shines through the
    tomb
  From the evergreen mountains of life.

The spirit-land is real and substantial—there souls eternally unfold.

We shall know and love each other there. Memory is the recording angel. Glorious will be the meeting of the loved in heaven, and grand the shout, "O death, where is thy sting? O grave, where is thy victory?"

It doth not yet appear what we shall be.

Spirits, remembering their own lives on earth, cherish deep and holy sympathies for humanity. Love never forgets. In the morning-time and the gray of evening, down golden-tided rivers sail these ministering spirits of God to catch the incense of each soul-felt prayer. They come to impress and inspire. Their magnetisms are baptisms, their words the spirit-echoes of eternal life.

None say in the Summer-Land of spirit-life, "I tread the wine-press alone," for the law of harmonial associations is there fully realized.

Beautiful and glorious are those homes of mutual love embowered in roses; those palaces of art tinged with electric light; those heavens of scientists, brotherhoods of philanthropists, and congresses of angels —*all* adding to the beatific glories of life in the republics of immortality.

PROGRESS AND THE VICTORY.

Creation, as a word expressive of the origin of things, is fast giving place to the terms formation and evolution. If something from nothing is an absolute impossibility, as it must be, then essential spirit, intermediate spirit substance, and gross matter are *all* necessarily eternal. Spirit *per se* is eternal force, or pure intelligence.

Spirit-substance is infinitely more refined and sublimated than physical matter; the qualities of which the senses to some degree cognize. Progress pertains to all things from sands to solar orbs, from atoms to angels, and evolution is the method of unfoldment.

Nature's kingdom admits of these general divisions: the mineral, the vegetable, the animal, the human, and the spiritual. While the mineral lies at the base of this mighty pyramid, the spiritual is the key-stone in the arch, the crowning glory of life's grand effort. Overarching and interpermeating all these kingdoms is the Infinite Presence, Essential Spirit, "God all, and in all."

Spirit and matter are coexistent and coeternal. Matter is constituted of atoms, which atoms in their myriad combinations are the centres from which force emanates. As much, if not more, is known of spirit than matter, that is, when matter is transformed from the solid to the gaseous, and further reduced to the last analysis, becoming invisible. All that is known of matter, whether solid, liquid, gaseous, or invisible, is through its qualities and forces. That is, as we learn of the rose by its color and fragrance, of the sun by means of its light, heat, and gravitation, so do we learn of the atom by its attraction, methods of combination, and other qualities. When we come in contact with a solid, it is not the atom we touch; we only touch the sphere of its emanating force.

Spirit, infilling, moulds and fashions material forms. The spirit in man is a portion of the Divine Intelligence. The spiritual body is composed of refined and etherealized essences—essences eliminated from foods and drinks; from atmospheres breathed and invisible auras appropriated. Death severs the copartnership existing between the physical and spiritual bodies. The physical body, serviceable to the spiritual for a season —as is chaff to wheat, and husks to growing corn— is raised again only in grasses, grains, and the fruits of autumn. The spiritual body, aflame with spirit, and a perfect structure self-balanced, becomes more ethereal and beautiful as the individual unfolds and advances in the morning-land of immortality. All the good, all the wisdom gained on earth is retained in the world of spirits.

Salvation is a process—a soul-growth—a blossoming and ripening up of the spiritual nature. It comes to nations and to individuals through the *Tau* of the Chinese; the *Buddha* of the Orientals; the *Logos* of John, and the *Christ* of the New Testament—comes as vegetation, flowers, and golden harvests come through the warmth and light of the sun. This Christ-principle is the "savor of life unto life"— the "morning star" of the Apocalypse. The pure in heart see God.

SPIRITUAL HYMNS

AND

SONGS.

THE EVERGREEN SHORE.

Page 164, *S. II.*

This world of strife is not our home;
  We're bound for the evergreen shore,
That land of beauty where loved ones have gone,
  Our loved ones, for evermore.

CHORUS.

Rest, rest! forever at home,
  Where pain and distress shall be o'er,
We yearn to be free in those realms to roam,
  Our home on the evergreen shore.

They beckon on our way along;
  We press for the evergreen shore;
We soon shall enter that heavenly throng,
  Where parting shall be no more.

CHORUS.

There fadeless garlands ever bloom
In paths on the evergreen shore,
Where pain and sickness, bereavement and gloom,
Shall mar our repose no more.

CHORUS.

LET THE GOOD ANGELS COME IN.

THEY hover around us, bright angels are near,
To glory immortal they win;
Then gladly we'll open the door of our hearts,
And let the good angels come in.
How kindly our Father has sent them to keep
A watch over His children below!
They're with us in slumber; their eyes never sleep;
They are with us wherever we go.

CHORUS.

Let them come in; let them come in;
Let the good angels come in, come in;
Let them come in; let them come in;
Let the good angels come in.
Come in, come in, —
Good angels, come in.

To comfort the lonely and strengthen the weak,
Their mission of mercy and love;
And oft on their beautiful pinions of light
They bear our petitions above.
Oh, let them come in! they are holy and pure!
Their presence how tenderly sweet!
They echo the song of the happy and blessed;
They learn at Immanuel's feet.

CHORUS.

OH, SING TO ME OF HEAVEN.

Oh, sing to me of heaven,
  When I am called to die;
Sing songs of holy ecstasy,
  To waft my soul on high.

Cho.—There'll be no more sorrow there,
  There'll be no more sorrow there;
In heav'n above, where all is love,
  There'll be no more sorrow there.

When cold and sluggish drops
  Roll off my marble brow;
Break forth in songs of joyfulness,
  Let heaven begin below.
    Chorus.

Then close the mortal eyes,
  And lay the form to rest,
And fold the pale and icy hands
  Upon the lifeless breast.
    Chorus.

Then to my raptured soul
  Let one sweet song be given;
Let music cheer me last on earth,
  And greet me first in heaven.
    Chorus.

A NEW RELIGION.

Air—Old Hundred.

1. A new religion shakes the earth,
  Christ, unbeknown to outward sage,
Descends in forms of love, to birth,
  And leads from heaven the golden age.

2. A new religion, new yet old,
   The Spirit's faith, the Eden theme,
   Descends the dreary earth to fold
   In joy transcending angel's dream.

3. Whence comes the light, whence comes the power,
   To burst the chains and break the rod?
   Whence comes the bright delivering hour?
   'Tis all of God, 'tis all of God!

COME, GENTLE SPIRITS.

Air—ORTONVILLE.

COME, gentle spirits, to us now,
  Look on with tender eyes;
Touch your soft hand upon each brow,
  Sweet spirits from the skies.

Come from your homes of perfect light,
  Come from your silvery streams,
Come from your scenes of joy more bright
  Than we e'er know in dreams.

Oh, speak to us in gentle tones!
  Our hearts are seeking now
A beauty like to that which shines
  Upon each angel's brow.

Like holy star-beams on a sea,
  Filled bright with happy isles,
Whence sullen storms forever flee,
  Where heaven forever smiles—

They come, and night is no more night,
  Pale sorrow's reign is o'er;
For death is but a gate of light,
  And gloomy now no more.

THE SHINING SHORE.

Page 400, *The Revivalist.*

My days are gliding swiftly by,
   And I, a pilgrim stranger,
Would not detain them as they fly !
   Those hours of toil and danger.

CHORUS.

For oh ! we stand on Jordan's strand
   Our friends are passing over,
And, just before, the shining shore
   By faith we now discover.

We'll gird our loins, my brethren dear,
   Our distant home discerning ;
Our absent Lord has left us word,
   " Let every lamp be burning."

Should coming days be cold and dark,
   We need not cease our singing ;
That perfect rest naught can molest,
   Where golden harps are ringing.

Let sorrow's rudest tempest blow,
   Each cord on earth to sever ;
Our loved say, come, and there's our home
   Forever, oh ! forever.

    CHO.—For oh ! we stand, etc.

THE BEAUTIFUL RIVER.

Page 258, *The Revivalist.*

Shall we gather at the river,
   Where bright angel feet have trod,
With its crystal tide forever
   Flowing by the throne of God ?

CHORUS—Yes, we'll gather at the river,
    The beautiful, the beautiful river,—
  Gather with our loved at the river,
    That flows by the throne of God.

On the margin of the river,
  Washing up its silver spray,
We will walk and worship ever
  All the happy golden day.
CHO.—Yes, we'll gather, etc.

Ere we reach the shining river,
  Lay we every burden down;
Truth our spirits will deliver,
  And provide us with a crown.
CHO.—Yes, we'll gather, etc.

Soon we'll reach the silver river,
  Soon our pilgrimage will cease;
Soon our happy hearts will quiver
  With the melody of peace.
CHO.—Yes, we'll gather, etc.

THE MORNING LIGHT.

Page 581, *The Revivalist.*

1. THE morning light is breaking,
    The darkness disappears;
  The sons of earth are waking
    To penitential tears.
  Each breeze that sweeps the ocean
    Brings tidings from afar,
  Of nations in commotion,
    Prepared to banish war.

2. Rich dews of grace come o'er us
    In many a gentle shower,
  And brighter scenes before us
    Are opening every hour.

  Each cry, to heaven going,
   Abundant answer brings,
  And heavenly gales are blowing,
   With peace upon their wings.

8. Blest river of salvation,
   Pursue thy onward way;
  Flow thou to every nation,
   Nor in thy richness stay.
  Stay not till all the lowly
   Triumphant reach their home;
  Stay not till all the holy
   Proclaim—" The Truth is come !

JOY TO THE WORLD.

Antioch.

Joy to the world—the darkness flies,
 Let earth with gladness sing.
The morning comes, o'er all the skies
 She waves her purple wing.

Joy to the world—for truth abounds,
 And " error withering dies."
In fragments hurled upon the ground,
 Her broken altar lies.

Joy to the world—for man is free,
 His broken fetters fall.
He scorns to bow again his knee
 At Superstition's call.

Joy to the world—the anthem be—
 A song of triumph sing,
" O Grave ! where is thy victory ?
 O Death ! where is thy sting ? "

NEARER, MY GOD, TO THEE.

Bethany.

1. Nearer, my God, to Thee,
    Nearer to Thee!
  E'en though it be a cross
    That raiseth me,
  Still all my song shall be,
  Nearer, my God, to Thee,
    Nearer to Thee.

2. Tho' like a wanderer,
    The sun gone down,
  Darkness comes over me,
    My rest a stone,
  Yet in my dreams I'd be,
  Nearer, my God, to Thee,
    Nearer to Thee.

3. Then let my way appear
    Steps unto heaven;
  All that Thou sendest me
    In mercy given;
  Angels to beckon me,
  Nearer, my God, to Thee,
    Nearer to Thee.

4. Or, if on joyful wing,
    Cleaving the sky,
  Sun, moon, and stars forgot,
    Upward I fly;
  Still all my song shall be,
  Nearer, my God, to Thee,
    Nearer to Thee.

ARE WE NOT BROTHERS ALL?

Coronation.

Hushed be the battle's fearful roar,
  The warriors' rushing call!

Why should the earth be drenched in gore?
Are we not brothers all?

Want from the starving poor depart!
Chains from the captive fall!
Great God, subdue the oppressor's heart!
Are we not brothers all?

Sect, clan, and dogma, oh! strike down—
Each mean partition wall,
Let love the voice of discord drown—
Are we not brothers all?

Let love and truth and peace alone
Hold tyranny in thrall,
That Heaven its work at length may own—
Are we not brothers all?

THE ENTERTAINING SIGHT.

Balerma.

1. Lo! what an entertaining sight
   Those friendly brethren prove,
   Whose cheerful hearts in bonds unite
   Of harmony and love.

2. What streams of bliss from angels spring,
   Baptizing every soul;
   What heavenly peace, with balmy wing,
   Shades and bedews the whole!

3. Aid us to help, with loving heart,
   Each other's cross to bear;
   Let each a friendly aid impart,
   And feel a brother's care.

4. Help us to build each other up,
   Our spirit gifts improve,
   Increase our faith, confirm our hope,
   And perfect us in love.

HOW CHEERING THE THOUGHT.

Edinburg.—S. Harp.

How cheering the thought, that the angels of God
Do bow their light wings to the world they once trod;
Do leave the sweet joys of the mansions above,
To breathe o'er our bosoms some message of love.

They come, on the wings of the morning they come,
Impatient to guide some poor wanderer home;
Some brother to lead from a darkened abode,
And lay him to rest in the arms of his God.

They come when we wander, they come when we pray,
In mercy to guard wherever we stray;
A glorious cloud, their bright witness is given;
Encircling us here, are these angels of heaven.

WELCOME, ANGELS.

Pleyel.

Welcome, angels pure and bright,
Children of the living light;
Welcome to our homes on earth,
Children of the glorious birth.

Welcome, messengers of God,
Teaching not of anger's rod;
Love for all earth's weary throng,
Is the burden of your song.

Come ye from the realms of light
Where the day knows not the night—
Where the gems of love alone
Are around your spirits thrown.

Oh, we joy to feel you near,
Spirits of the loved and dear;
Chains of love around us twine,
Gems of beauty, all divine.

THE TIE OF BROTHERHOOD.

Boylston.

BLEST be the tie that binds
  Our hearts in holy love;
The fellowship of kindred minds
  Is like to that above.

We share our mutual woes,
  Our mutual burdens bear,
And often for each other flows
  The sympathizing tear.

When we asunder part,
  It gives us inward pain;
But we shall still be joined in heart,
  And gladly meet again.

This glorious hope revives
  Our courage by the way;
While each in expectation lives,
  And longs to see the day.

THE EDEN ABOVE.

Music—S. Harp.

WE'RE bound for the land of the pure and the holy,
  The home of the happy, the kingdom of love.
Ye wand'rers from God in the broad road of folly,
  Oh, say, will you go to the Eden above?
CHO.—Will you go, will you go, will you go?
      Oh, say, will you go to the Eden above?

In that blessed land neither sighing nor anguish
  Can breathe in the fields where the glorified rove.
Ye heart-burdened ones, who in misery languish,
  Oh, say, will you go to the Eden above?
  CHORUS.

No poverty there, no, the good are all wealthy—
The heirs of His glory whose nature is love ;
Nor sickness can reach them, that country is healthy,
Oh, say, will you go to the Eden above ?
CHORUS.

March on, happy pilgrims, that land is before you,
And soon its ten thousand delights we shall prove ;
Yes, soon we shall walk o'er the hills of bright glory,
And drink the pure joys of the Eden above.
CHORUS.

SWEET BY-AND-BY.

THERE'S a land that is fairer than day,
And by faith we may see it afar,
For the angels wait over the way,
To prepare us a dwelling-place there.

CHORUS.
In the sweet by-and-by
We shall meet on that beautiful shore,
In the sweet by-and-by
We shall meet on that beautiful shore.

We shall sing on that beautiful shore,
The melodious songs of the blest,
And our spirits shall sorrow no more,
Not a sigh for the blessings of rest.

CHORUS.—In the sweet, etc.

To our bountiful Father above,
We will offer the tribute of praise,
For the glorious gift of His love,
And the blessings that hallow our days.

CHORUS.—In the sweet, etc.

BRIGHT HILLS OF GLORY.

Page 155, *S. Harp.*

Oh, give me a harp on the bright hills of glory,
 A home when life's sorrows are o'er,
Where joys that awaken the meek and the lowly
 Will more than famed Eden restore.

CHORUS.

Where the new song is giv'n
 To the loved ones in heav'n,
And the angels re-echo the song,
 When the new song is giv'n
To the loved ones in heav'n,
And the angels re-echo the song.

Oh, there let me roam on the banks of the river,
 Escorted by angels along,
And with them adore the bounteous Giver,
 Whose love is rehearsed by the throng.

CHORUS.

There sweetly we'll rest in those mansions forever,
 And bask in the fulness of love ;
Where fields are all bright with flow'rets that never
 Shall wither in Eden above.

CHORUS.

HOME, SWEET HOME.

Though far o'er the wide earth our footsteps may
  roam,
The soul ever pants for its glorious home,
It turns from the earth with its treasures and gems,
To heaven, and longs for its glorious realms.
 Home, home, sweet, sweet home,
The soul ever pants for its glorious home.

Earth's waters of mirth and of pleasure may roll,
Still, still, there's a void in the depth of the soul;
It feels that its joys are not sacred and true,
If 'tis not refreshed by its home's purest dew.
 Home, home, sweet, sweet home,
The soul ever pants for its glorious home.

When crowds gather round and earth's revels run high,
The glare of excitement may light up the eye,
But dimmed would its sight be when dark sorrows come,
If the soul should reflect not the light of its home.
 Home, home, sweet, sweet home,
The soul ever pants for its glorious home.

When the soul bursts its chains, e'en the cold, glazing eye
Betokens its rapture while soaring on high,
The soul, as it flies to the angels' embrace,
Flings one lingering beam from its home o'er the face.
 Home, home, sweet, sweet home.
The soul ever pants for its glorious home.

PROTECTING POWER.

Brattle Street, Page 60, P. of L.

WHILE Thee I seek, protecting Power!
 Be my vain wishes stilled,
And may this consecrated hour
 With better hopes be filled.
Thy love the power of thought bestowed,
 To thee my thoughts would soar:
Thy mercy o'er my life has flowed;
 That mercy I adore.

In each event of life, how clear
 Thy ruling hand I see!
Each blessing to my soul more **dear**
 Because conferred by Thee.

In every joy that crowns my days,
  In every pain I bear,
My heart shall find delight in praise,
  Or seek relief in prayer.

When gladness wings my favored hour,
  Thy love my thoughts shall fill;
Resigned when storms of sorrow lower,
  My soul shall meet Thy will.
My lifted eye without a tear
  The gathering storm shall see;
My steadfast heart shall know no fear,
  That heart shall rest on thee.

REST FOR THE WEARY.

S. Harp

In the angels' home in glory,
  There remains a land of rest,
There the loved have gone before us
  To fulfill our soul's request.

CHORUS.

There is rest for the weary,
There is rest for the weary,
There is rest for the weary,
  There is rest for you.
On the other side of Jordan,
In the sweet fields of Eden,
Where the tree of life is blooming,
  There is rest for you.

They are fitting up our mansion,
  Which eternally shall stand,
For our stay shall not be transient
  In that holy, happy land.
  CHORUS.

Pain nor sickness ne'er shall enter,
  Grief nor woe our lot shall share;

But in that celestial centre
  Each a crown of life shall wear.
  CHORUS.

Death itself shall then be vanquished,
  And his sting shall be withdrawn;
Shout for gladness, oh, ye ransomed!
  Hail with joy the rising morn.
  CHORUS.

THE BEAUTIFUL LAND.

Page 295, *L. Manual.*

A BEAUTIFUL land of joy I see —
A land of rest, from sorrow free,
The home of the spirit, bright and fair;
And loving hearts are beating there.
  Will you go? Will you go?
  Go to that beautiful land with me?
  Will you go? Will you go?
  Go to that beautiful land?

That beautiful land, the land of light,
Has never known the shades of night;
The sunbright glow of endless day
Hath driven the darkness far away.
  Will you go? Will you go? etc.

In vision I see the shining shore,
The flowers that bloom for evermore;
The river of life, the crystal sea,
The ambrosial fruit of life's fair tree.
  Will you go? Will you go? etc.

The heavenly throng, arrayed in white,
In rapture range the plains of light;
In one harmonious choir they raise
To Nature's God a song of praise.
  Will you go? Will you go? etc.

OUR LOVED IN HEAVEN.

Page 152, *S. Harp.*

Come, all ye loved, to wisdom's mountain,
   Come, view your home beyond the tide,
Hear now the voices of the angels,
   Singing so sweet the other side;
Some are singing of bright palms of glory,
   Some of dear ones who stand near the shore;
For the fond heart must ever be clinging
   To the faithful we love evermore.

CHORUS.

Oh, the prospect! it is so transporting,
   And no danger I fear from the tide;
Let me go to the home of the angels,
   Let me stand robed in white by their side

There endless streams of light are flowing,
   There are the fields of living bloom,
Mansions of beauty are provided,
   Open to all beyond the tomb.
Soon my conflicts and toils will be ended,
   I shall join those who've passed on before,
For my loved ones, oh, how I do miss them!
   I'll press on there to meet them once more.

CHORUS.

Faith now beholds the flowing river,
   Coming from that celestial shore;
There, the departed live forever,
   Live there immortal evermore.
Would you sit by the banks of the river
   With the friends you have loved by your side?
Would you join in the song of the angels?
   Then be ready to follow your guide.

CHORUS.

THERE IS JOY FOR YOU.

Page 170, *S. Harp*

Oh! let not your hearts be troubled,
  Neither let them be afraid,
For behold the Bridegroom cometh
  In His wedding robes arrayed.

CHORUS.

There is joy for the faithful,
There is joy for the faithful,
There is joy for the faithful,
  There is joy for you.
In the higher land of wisdom,
Where the angels sing for glory,
Far beyond death's rolling river,
  There is joy for you.

Deeply drink of love celestial
  From the fountain flowing free,
For it giveth joy forever,—
  Joy o'er all that crystal sea.
    CHORUS.

Tell me not, ye weary laden,
  There is naught but sorrow here,
For the angels are descending
  To remove earth's blighting fear.
    CHORUS.

Keep your minds in truth-light burning!
  Walk in virtue's humble way,
And be ready for your exit
  To the realms of perfect day.
    CHORUS.

HAND IN HAND WITH ANGELS.

Page 155, *P. of Life*

Hand in hand with angels,
  Through the world we go;

Brighter eyes are on us
  Than we blind ones know
Tenderer voices cheer us
  Than we deaf will own ;
Never, walking heavenward,
  Can we walk alone.

Hand in hand with angels,
  Some are out of sight,
Leading us, unknowing,
  Into paths of light ;
Some soft hands are covered
  From our mortal clasp,
Soul in soul to hold us
  With a firmer clasp.

Hand in hand with angels,
  Walking every day,
How the chain may brighten
  None of us can say ;
Yet it doubtless reaches
  From earth's lowest one
To the loftiest seraph
  Standing near the throne.

Hand in hand with angels,
  Ever let us go ;
Clinging to the strong ones,
  Drawing up the slow.
One electric love-stone,
  Thrilling all with fire,
Soar we through vast ages,
  Higher—ever higher.

THE BEAUTIFUL.

C. M. D.—Page 80, *P. of Life.*

The world has much of beautiful,
  If man would only see ;
A glory in the beaming stars,
  The lowest budding tree ;

A splendor from the farthest east
  Unto the farthest west;
Aye! everything is beautiful,
  And we are greatly blest.

There is a host of angels, who
  With every moment throng,
If we could only list a while
  The cadence of their song;
They speak in every sunny glance
  That flashes on the stream,
In every holy thrill of ours,
  And every lofty dream.

The world is good and beautiful,
  We all may know it well,
For there are many thousand tongues
  That every day can tell
What love has cheered them on their way,
  O'er every ill above—
It only needs a goodly heart
  To know that all is love!

SHERBURNE

Page 90, *The Revivalist.*

WHILE shepherds watch'd their flocks by night,
  All seated on the ground,
The angel of the Lord came down,
  And glory shone around.

"Fear not," said he (for mighty dread
  Had seized their troubled mind),
"Glad tidings of great joy I bring,
  To you and all mankind.

"To you, in David's town, this day
  Is born, of David's line,
A Teacher, who is Christ the Lord,
  And this shall be the sign:

"The heavenly Babe you there shall find
  To human view display'd,
All meanly wrapp'd in swathing bands,
  And in a manger laid."

Thus spake the seraph; and forthwith
  Appear'd a shining throng
Of angels, praising God on high,
  And thus address'd their song:

"All glory be to God on high,
  And to the earth be peace;
Good-will henceforth from heaven to men
  Begin and never cease."

DREAMING TO-NIGHT.

Page 64, The Revivalist, or Page 176 S. H.

WE'RE dreaming to-night of the loved ones dear
  Gone to the summer-land;
We pine for the smiles and the tones so sweet,
  And the clasp of a gentle hand.

CHORUS.

Weary are our hearts as we gather to-night,
  Sighing o'er our broken chain,
Longing for the gift of a clearer sight
  To see our loved again;
Dreaming to-night, dreaming to-night,
Dreaming of the loved ones dear.

We're dreaming to-night of the loved ones dear,
  Yonder a vacant chair
Seems filled with a form, ever beloved and revered,
  Crowned with halo of silv'ry hair.
      CHORUS.

We're dreaming to-night of the loved ones dear;
  Many a beaming face
Of friend and companion our fancies woo
  To its old accustomed place.
      CHORUS.

EXALTATION

Lenox, H. M.—Page 110, *P. of Life.*

Ye realms below the skies,
   The Father's praises sing ;
Let boundless honors rise
   To heaven's eternal King·
Oh, bless His name whose love extends
Salvation to the world's far ends.

'Tis He the mountain crowns
   With forests waving wide ;
'Tis He old ocean bounds,
   And heaves her roaring tide ;
He swells the tempests on the main,
Or breathes the zephyr o'er the plain.

Still let the waters roar
   As round the earth they roll ;
His praise for evermore
   They sound from pole to pole.
'Tis Nature's wild, unconscious song
O'er thousand waves that floats along.

His praise, ye worlds on high,
   Display with all your spheres,
Amid the darksome sky,
   When silent night appears.
Behold, His works declare His name
Through all the universal frame.

THE BOWER OF PRAYER.

Page 345, *The Revivalist.*

To leave my dear friends and with neighbors to part,
And go from my home, it affects not my heart
Like the thought of absenting myself for a day
From that blest retreat where I've chosen to pray ;
   Where I've chosen to pray.

Sweet bower, where the pine and the poplar have spread,
And woven their branches a roof o'er my head;
How oft have I knelt on the evergreen there,
And poured out my soul to the angels in prayer.

The early shrill notes of a loved nightingale,
That dwelt in my bower, I observed as my bell
To call me to duty, while birds in the air
Sung anthems of praises as I went to prayer.

How sweet were the zephyrs perfumed with the pine,
The ivy, the balsam, the wild eglantine!
But sweeter, oh! sweeter, superlative were
The joys that I tasted in answer to prayer.

Sweet bower, I must leave you and bid you adieu,
And pay my devotions in parts that are new;
Well knowing that Jesus resides everywhere,
And will in all places give answer to prayer.

I'M A PILGRIM.

Page 450, *The Revivalist.*

I'm a pilgrim and I'm a stranger,
I can tarry, I can tarry but a night;
Do not detain me, for I am going
To where the streamlets are ever flowing.

Of that city, to which I journey,
My Redeemer, my Redeemer is the light,
There is no sorrow, nor any sighing,
Nor any tears, nor any dying.

There the sunbeams are ever shining,
Oh! my longing heart, my longing heart is there;
Here in this country, so dark and dreary,
I long have wandered forlorn and weary.

Farewell, dreary earth, by sin so blighted,
In immortal beauty soon you'll be arrayed,
For He who formed thee will soon restore thee,
From sin and death to praise and glory.

SHALL WE KNOW EACH OTHER THERE?

Page 472, The Revivalist.

WHEN we hear the music ringing,
   In the bright celestial dome,
When sweet angel voices singing,
   Gladly bid us welcome home
To the land of ancient story,
   Where the spirit knows no care,
In that land of light and glory,
   Shall we know each other there?

When the holy angels meet us,
   As we go to join their band,
Shall we know the friends that greet us
   In the glorious spirit-land?
Shall we see the same eyes shining
   On us as in days of yore?
Shall we feel their dear arms twining
   Fondly round us, as before?

Yes, my earth-worn soul rejoices,
   And my weary heart grows light,
For the thrilling angel voices
   And the angel faces bright
That shall welcome us in heaven
   Are the loved of long ago,
And to them 'tis kindly given
   Thus their mortal friends to know.

Oh! ye weary, sad, and toss'd ones,
   Droop not, faint not by the way;
Ye shall join the lov'd and just ones
   In the land of perfect day!

Harp-strings touched by angel fingers
  Murmured in my raptured ear,
Evermore their sweet song lingers:
  "We shall know each other there."

THE BRIGHT LAND OF BEULAH.

Page 169, *The Revivalist*

My latest sun is sinking fast,
  My race is nearly run;
My strongest trials now are past,
  My triumph is begun.

CHORUS.

  Oh, come, angel band,
  Come and around me stand
Oh, bear me away on your snowy wings,
  To my immortal home.
Oh, bear me away on your snowy wings,
  To my immortal home.

I know I'm nearing the holy ranks
  Of friends and kindred dear,
For I brush the dews on Jordan's banks,
  The crossing must be near.

CHORUS.

I've almost gained my heavenly home,
  My spirit loudly sings;
The holy ones, behold, they come!
  I hear the noise of wings.

CHORUS.

Oh, bear my longing heart to Him
  Who loved and cared for me;
Whose truth now cleanses from all sin,
  And gives us victory.

CHORUS.

SWEET HOUR OF PRAYER.

Page 157, *The Revivalist.*

Sweet hour of prayer! sweet hour of prayer!
That calls me from a world of care,
And bids me on my Father's throne
Make all my wants and wishes known.
In seasons of distress and grief
My soul has often found relief,
And oft escaped the tempter's snare,
By thy return, sweet hour of prayer.

Sweet hour of prayer! sweet hour of prayer!
Thy wings shall my petition bear
To Him whose truth and faithfulness
Engage the waiting soul to bless;
And since He bids me seek His face,
Believe His word and trust His grace,
I'll cast on Him my every care,
And wait for thee, sweet hour of prayer!

Sweet hour of prayer! sweet hour of prayer!
May I thy consolation share,
Till from Mount Pisgah's lofty height
I view my home and take my flight!
This robe of flesh I'll drop and rise
To seize the everlasting prize;
And shout while passing thro' the air,
Farewell, farewell, sweet hour of prayer!

THE EDEN OF LOVE.

Page 253, *The Revivalist.*

How sweet to reflect on those joys that await me
  In yon blissful region, the haven of rest,
Where glorified spirits, with welcome shall greet me,
  And lead me to mansions prepared for the blest.
Encircled in light and with glory enshrouded,
  My happiness perfect, my mind's sky unclouded,
I'll bathe in the ocean of pleasure unbounded,
  And range with delight thro' the Eden of Love.

While angelic legions, with harps tuned celestial,
  Harmoniously join in the concert of praise,
The saints, as they flock from the regions terrestrial,
  In loud hallelujahs their voices shall raise;
Then songs to the Lamb shall re-echo through heaven,
  My soul will respond: "To Immanuel be given
All glory, all honor, all might and dominion,
  Who brought us through grace to the Eden of Love.'

Then hail, blessed state! Hail, ye songsters of glory
  Ye harpers of bliss, soon I'll meet you above,
And join your full choir in rehearsing the story,
  Salvation from sorrow, thro' Jesus' love.
Though prisoned in earth, yet by anticipation,
  Already my soul feels a sweet prelibation
Of joys that await me, when freed from probation;
  My heart's now in heaven, the Eden of Love!

THE PILGRIM STRANGER.

Page 370, *The Revivalist.*

WHITHER goest thou, pilgrim stranger,
  Wandering through this gloomy vale,
Knowest thou not 'tis full of danger,
  And will not thy courage fail?

CHORUS.

No, I'm bound for the kingdom;
  Will you go to glory with me?
Halle-lu-jah! Praise ye the Lord!

Pilgrim thou hast justly call'd me,
  Passing through the waste so wide,
But no harm will e'er befall me
  While I'm blest with such a Guide.
        CHORUS.

Such a guide! no guide attends thee,
  Hence for thee my fears arise;

SPIRITUAL HARMONIES. 45

If some guardian power befriend thee
'Tis unseen by mortal eyes.
CHORUS.

Yes, unseen, but still believe me,
Such a Guide my steps attends;
He'll in every strait relieve me,
He will Guide me to the end.
CHORUS.

Pilgrim, see that stream before thee,
Darkly winding through the vale;
Should its deadly waves roll o'er thee
Would not then thy courage fail?
CHORUS.

No, that stream has nothing frightful,
To its brink my steps I'll bend,
Thence to plunge 'twill be delightful,
There my pilgrimage will end.
CHORUS.

WHEN SHALL WE MEET AGAIN?

Page 437, *The Revivalist.*

WHEN shall we meet again—
Meet ne'er to sever?
When will peace wreathe her chain
Round us forever?
Our hearts will ne'er repose,
Safe from each blast that blows
In this dark vale of woes—
Never—no, never!

When shall love freely flow
Pure as life's river?
When shall sweet friendship glow
Changeless forever?

Where joys celestial thrill,
Where bliss each heart shall fill,
And fears of parting chill
  Never — no, never!

Up to that world of light
  Take us, dear angels!
May we all there unite,
  Happy forever;
Where kindred spirits dwell,
There may our music swell,
And time our joys dispel
  Never — no, never'

AMERICA.

Page 65, *S. H.*

My country, 'tis of thee,
Sweet land of liberty,
  Of thee I sing;
Land where our fathers died,
Land of the pilgrims' pride,
From every mountain-side
  Let freedom ring.

My native country, thee,
Land of the noble free,
  Thy name I love.
I love thy rocks and rills,
Thy woods and templed hills;
My heart with rapture thrills
  Like that above.

Let music swell the breeze,
And ring from all the trees
  Sweet freedom's song!
Let mortal tongues awake,
Let all that breathe partake,
Let rocks their silence break,
  The sound prolong.

WE LOVE THE FATHER.

Page 62, *L. G.*

We love the Father, He's so good;
    We see Him in the flower,
We hear Him in the rain-drop,
    He speaketh in the shower;
His smile is in the sunlight,
    His beauty in the bow;
We hear His whisper in the breeze,
    And in the zephyr low.

His wisdom's in the dew-drop
    That sparkles on the lea,
His truth is in the violet's hue,
    His love's in all we see.
He's merciful and kind to all,
    And ever just and true;
To those who truly on Him call
    He ever gives their due.

Oh, may we ever gentle be
    In all our works and ways,
In all our conduct frank and free,
    And His great goodness praise.
In everything we look upon,
    His image we can see.
We love the Father, He's so good,
    And teaches us to be.

THE MISSIONARY HYMN.

From Greenland's icy mountains,
    From India's coral strand,
Where Afric's sunny fountains
    Roll down their golden sand;
From many an ancient river,
    From many a palmy plain,
They call us to deliver
    Their land from error's chain.

Lift up thy face to heaven;
　In God Messiah's ray
Thy mystic night is riven,
　Thou beautiful Cathay!
Flow forth in balms and spices,
　Ye gardens of the blest!
From Osiris and Isis
　Egyptia findeth rest.

Thou, too, awake from slumber,
　Clime of the Muses' throne!
No idols shall encumber
　Thy new-found Parthenon.
Serene and luminescent,
　Glad Islam, rise, behold
The cross above the crescent,
　Enshrined in spirit-gold.

From every land shall gather
　Returning Judah's host,
And own the loved All-Father,
　At Zion's Pentecost.
From nation unto nation,
　Ye glorious voices, roll,
And speed regeneration,
　To every living soul.

FOOTSTEPS OF ANGELS.

Greenville.

When the hours of day are numbered,
　And the voices of the night
Wake the better soul that slumbered
　To a holy, calm delight,

Ere the evening lamps are lighted,
　And like phantoms grim and tall
Shadows from the fitful firelight
　Dance upon the parlor wall;

Then the forms of the departed
  Enter at the open door;
The beloved ones, the true-hearted,
  Come to visit me once more.

With a slow and noiseless footstep
  Come the messengers divine,
Take the vacant chair beside me,
  Lay their gentle hands in mine;

And they sit and gaze upon me
  With those deep and tender eyes,
Like the stars, so still and saint-like,
  Looking downward from the skies.

Uttered not, yet comprehended,
  Is the spirit's voiceless prayer;
Soft rebukes in blessings ended,
  Breathing from their lips of air.

VOICES FROM THE SPIRIT-LAND.

Page 136, *P. of L.*

In the silence of the midnight,
  When the cares of day are o'er,
In my soul I hear the voices
  Of the loved ones gone before;
Hear them words of comfort whisp'ring,
  That they'll watch on every hand·
And I love, I love to list to
  Voices from the spirit-land.

In my wanderings oft there cometh
  Sudden stillness to my soul,
When around, above, within it,
  Rapturous joys unnumbered roll;
Though around me all is tumult,
  Noise and strife on every hand,
Yet within my soul I list to
  Voices from the spirit-land.

Loved ones that have gone before me,
  Whisper words of peace and joy;
Those that long since have departed,
  Tell me their divine employ
Is to watch and guard my footsteps;
  Oh, it is an angel-band!
And my soul is cheered in hearing
  Voices from the spirit-land.

ANGEL FRIENDS.

Page 126, *P. of Life.*

Floating on the breath of evening,
  Breathing in the morning prayer,
Hear we oft the the tender voices
  That once made our world so fair.

We forget, while listening to them,
  All the sorrows we have known,
And upon the troubles present,
  Faith's pure, shining light is thrown.

Soothing with their magic whispers,
  Calming all our wildest fears;
Thus they bring us sweet submission—
  Peace for sorrow, smiles for tears.

Bless you, angel friends, oh, never
  Leave us lonely on the way!
For your gentle teachings ever
  Meekly may we watch and pray.

MY ANGEL NAME.

Music by James G. Clark.

In the land where I am going,
  When my early life is o'er,
When the tired hands cease their striving,
  And the tired heart aches no more, —
In that land of light and beauty,
  Where no shadow ever came
To o'ercloud the perfect glory,
  What shall be my angel name?

When the spirits who await me
  Meet me at my entering in,
With what name of love and music
  Will their welcoming begin?
Not the one so dimmed with earth-stains,
  Linked with thoughts of grief and shame;
No! the name that mortals gave me
  Will not be my angel name!

I have heard it all too often
  Uttered by unloving lips;
Earthly care, and sin and sorrow,
  Dim it with their deep eclipse.
I shall change it like a garment
  When I leave this mortal frame,
And at life's immortal baptism
  I shall have another name.

For the angels will not call me
  By the name I bear on earth;
They will speak a holier language
  Where I have my holier birth;
Syllabled in heavenly music,
  Sweeter far than earth may claim,
Very gentle, pure, and tender, —
  Such will be my angel name.

It has thrilled my spirit often
   In the holiest of my dreams;
But its beauty lingers with me
   Only like the morning beams.
Weary of the jarring discord
   Which the lips of mortals frame,
When shall I, with joy and rapture,
   Answer to my angel name?

CELESTIAL GREETINGS.

T. L. Harris.

Peace be thine, the angels greet thee.
   Kindred spirit, welcome here!
In their blissful calm they meet thee —
   Shed abroad their loving sphere.
Enter, then, the sacred portals;
   Here thy heart's pure homage pay;
For the beautiful immortals
   Worship in our midst to-day.

With us all the meek-voiced angels
   Reverent and adoring stand,
While we hear divine evangels
   From the soul's great fatherland.
Oh! though sorrow's chain hath bound us,
   All our grief shall pass away;
For the Father's hand hath crowned us
   In his glorious courts to-day.

THE DEEDS OF CHARITY.

C. M.

The man of charity extends
   To all a liberal hand;
His kindred, neighbors, foes, and friends,
   His pity may command.

He aids the poor in their distress,
　He hears when they complain;
With tender heart delights to bless,
　And lessen all their pain.

The sick, the prisoner, poor and blind,
　And all the sons of grief,
In him a benefactor find;
　He loves to give relief.

Then let us all in love abound,
　And charity pursue;
Thus shall we be with glory crowned,
　And love as angels do.

PRAYER.

C. M.

Prayer is the soul's sincere desire,
　Unuttered or expressed;
The motion of a hidden fire
　That trembles in the breast.

Prayer is the burden of a sigh,
　The falling of a tear,
The upward glancing of an eye,
　When none but God is near.

Prayer is the simplest form of speech
　That infant lips can try;
Prayer, the sublimest strains that reach
　The Majesty on high.

Prayer is the contrite sinner's voice,
　Returning from his ways;
While angels in their songs rejoice,
　And cry, "Behold he prays!"

HOME OF THE SOUL.

I will sing you a song of that beautiful land,
    The far-away home of the soul,
Where no storms ever beat on the glittering strand,
    While years of eternity roll.
        Where no storms, etc.

Oh, that home of the soul in my visions and dreams,
    Its bright jasper walls I can see;
Till I fancy but thinly the veil intervenes
    Between the fair city and me.
        Till I fancy, etc.

That unchangeable home is for you and for me,
    Where Jesus of Nazareth stands;
The King of all kingdoms forever is He,
    And He holdeth our crowns in his hands.
        The king of, etc.

Oh, how sweet it will be in that beautiful land,
    So free from all sorrow and pain,
With songs on our lips, and with harps in our hands,
    To meet one another again!
        With songs on, etc.

DARLING NELLY GRAY.

There's a low, green valley on the old Kentucky shore,
    Where I've whiled many happy hours away,
A-sitting and a-singing by the little cottage-door,
    Where lived my darling Nelly Gray.
Oh, my poor Nelly Gray, they have taken you away,
    And I'll never see my darling any more!
I'm sitting by the river, and I'm weeping all the day,
    For you've gone from the old Kentucky shore!

One night I went to see her; but "She's gone!" the
    neighbors say:
The white man bound her with his chain:
They have taken her to Georgia, to wear her life
    away,
    As she toils in the cotton and the cane.
        CHORUS. — Oh, my poor Nelly Gray, etc.

My canoe is under water, and my banjo is unstrung;
    I'm tired of living any more;
My eyes shall look downward, and my songs shall
    be unsung,
    While I stay on the old Kentucky shore.
        CHORUS. — Oh, my poor Nelly Gray, etc.

My eyes are getting blinded, and I cannot see my
    way;
Hark! there's somebody knocking at the door! —
Oh, I hear the angels calling, and I see my Nelly
    Gray!
    Farewell to the old Kentucky shore!
Oh, my darling Nelly Gray, up in heaven there, they
    say
That they'll never take you from me any more!
I'm a-coming, coming, coming, as the angels clear
    the way!
    Farewell to the old Kentucky shore!

LORD, DISMISS US.

Sicily.

LORD, dismiss us with thy blessing;
    Fill our hearts with joy and peace;
Let us each, thy love possessing,
    Triumph in redeeming grace.
        Oh, refresh us,
Travelling through this wilderness!

Thanks we give, and adoration,
  For thy gospel's joyful sound;
May the fruits of thy salvation
  In our hearts and lives abound;
    May thy presence
With us evermore be found.

So, whene'er the signal's given
  Us from earth to call away,
Borne on angels' wings to heaven,
  Glad the summons to obey,
    May we ever
Reign with Christ in endless day.

EQUALITY.

C. M.   *H. Martineau.*

ALL men are equal in their birth,
  Heirs of the earth and skies;
All men are equal when that earth
  Fades from their dying eyes.

Yet man *some inwrought* difference sees,
  And speaks of high and low,
And worships those, and tramples these,
  While the same path they go.

Oh, let man hasten to restore
  To all their rights of love!
In power and wealth exult no more;
  In wisdom lowly move.

Ye great, renounce your earth-born pride!
  Ye low, your shame and fear!
Live, as ye *suffer*, side by side:
  Your brotherhood revere!

WHEN SHALL WE ALL MEET AGAIN?

When shall we all meet again?
When shall we all meet again?
Oft shall glowing hope expire,
Oft shall wearied love retire,
Oft shall death and sorrow reign,
Ere we all shall meet again.

Though in distant lands we sigh,
Parched beneath a burning sky;
Though the deep between us rolls,
Friendship shall unite our souls;
And in fancy's wide domain
Oft shall we all meet again.

When these burnished locks are gray,
Thinned by many a toil-spent day;
When around this youthful pine
Moss shall creep and ivy twine,
(Long may this loved bower remain!)
Here may we all meet again.

When the dreams of life are fled,
When its wasted lamps are dead;
When in cold oblivion's shade
Beauty, wealth, and fame are laid,
Where immortal spirits reign
There may we all meet again.

GOD IS FOREVER WITH MAN.

P. M.

Heirs of the morning, we walk in the light;
   God is forever with man!
A day that hath never a noon or a night;
   God is forever with man!

A day without limit, whose glories unfold
The statutes that time and eternity hold;
An endless becoming its measure and mould:
   God is forever with man!

He sitteth a guest in humanity's soul;
   God is forever with man!
Life leadeth on to an infinite goal;
   God is forever with man!
Inward, not outward, is Deity's shrine,
The Presence eternal, the Spirit divine,
And being becomes immortality's sign:
   God is forever with man!

Of all that is real the human hath part;
   God is forever with man!
Our roots are the veins of the infinite heart;
   God is forever with man!
The Christ liveth ever in creature disguise;
The Logos by which every soul shall arise
To the gospel and glory of self-sacrifice;
   God is forever with man!

PILGRIM'S HAPPY LOT.

No foot of land do I possess;
No cottage in this wilderness;
   A poor wayfaring man.
I lodge awhile in tents below,
Or gladly wander to and fro,
   Till I my Canaan gain.

Nothing on earth I call my own;
A stranger to the world, unknown,
   I all their goods despise;
I trample on their whole delight,
And seek a city out of sight,
   A city in the skies.

There is my house and portion fair;
My treasure and my heart are there,
  And my abiding home;
For me my elder brethren stay,
And angels beckon me away,
  And Jesus bids me come.

I come, thy servant, Lord, replies;
I come to meet thee in the skies,
  And claim my heavenly rest;
Now let the pilgrim's journey end,
Now, O my Saviour, Brother, Friend,
  Receive me to thy breast!

WHERE THE ROSES NE'ER SHALL WITHER.

James G. Clark

WHERE the roses ne'er shall wither,
Nor the clouds of sorrow gather,
  We shall meet,
  We shall meet,
Where no wintry storm can roll,
Driving summer from the soul,
Where all hearts are tuned to love,
On that happy shore above.

CHORUS.

Where the roses ne'er shall wither,
Nor the clouds of sorrow gather,
Angel bands will guide us thither,
Where the roses ne'er shall wither.

Where the hills are ever vernal,
And the springs of youth eternal,
  We shall meet,
  We shall meet,

Where life's morning dream returns,
And the noonday never burns,
Where the dew of life is love,
On that happy shore above.
   CHORUS.

Where no cruel word is spoken,
Where no faithful heart is broken,
  We shall meet,
  We shall meet,
Hand in hand and heart to heart,
Friend with friend no more to part;
Ne'er to grieve for those we love,
On that happy shore above.
   CHORUS.

I'M HAPPY.

Revivalist.

I'm happy, I'm happy! O wondrous account!
My joys are immortal; I stand on the mount.
I gaze on my treasure, and long to be there,
With loved ones and angels, my kindred so dear.

O heaven! sweet heaven! I long to be gone
To meet all my brethren before the white throne!
Come angels! come angels! I'm ready to fly!
Come, quickly convey me to God up on high!

A glimpse of bright glory surprises my soul;
I sink in sweet visions to view the bright goal;
My soul, while I'm singing, is leaping to go;
This moment, for heaven I'd leave all below.

My soul's full of glory, inspiring my tongue;
Could I sing like angels, I'd sing them a song;
I'd sing of the Father, and tell of his charms,
And beg them to bear me to his loving arms.

ROYAL PROCLAMATION.

Hear the royal proclamation,
The glad tidings of salvation,
Published now to every creature,
To the erring sons of nature.

Chorus.

Lo! He reigns, He reigns victorious,
Over heaven and earth most glorious;
Jesus reigns.

See the royal banner flying;
Hear the heralds loudly crying;
Blinded sinners, royal favor
Now is offered by the Saviour.

Chorus.

Here are wine, and milk, and honey;
Come and purchase without money;
Mercy, like a flowing fountain,
Streaming from the holy mountain.

Chorus.

For this love let rocks and mountains,
Purling streams and crystal fountains,
Roaring thunders, lightning blazes,
Shout the great Eternal's praises.

Chorus.

THE SWEET STORY.

Revivalist.

1 I think, when I read that sweet story of old,
  When Jesus was here among men,
How He called little children as lambs to his fold,
  I should like to have been with them then.

I wish that his hands had been placed on my head;
  That his arms had been thrown around me;
And that I might have seen his kind look when he
    said,
  Let the little ones come unto me.

Yet still to his footstool in prayer I may go,
  And ask for a share in his love;
And if I thus earnestly seek Him below,
  I shall see Him and hear Him above.

In that beautiful place He is gone to prepare,
  Where all shall be loved and forgiven;
And many dear children are gathering there,
  For such is the kingdom of heaven.

THERE'S A LAND FAR AWAY.

James G. Clark.

There's a land far away 'mid the stars, we are told,
  Where they know not the sorrows of time;
Where the pure waters flow through the valleys of
    gold,
  And where life is a treasure sublime.
'Tis the land of our God, 'tis the home of the soul,
Where the ages of splendor eternally roll;
Where the way-weary traveller reaches his goal,
  On the ever-green mountains of life.

Here our gaze cannot soar to that beautiful land,
  But our visions have told of its bliss;
And our souls by the gale from its gardens are fanned,
  When we faint in the deserts of this.
And we sometimes have longed for its holy repose
When our hearts have been rent with temptations and
    woes,
And we've drank from the tide of the river that flows
  From the ever-green mountains of life.

Oh, the stars never tread the blue heavens at night
  But we think where the ransomed have trod;
And the day never smiles from his palace of light
  But we feel the bright smile of our God.
We are travelling home through earth's changes and gloom,
To a region where pleasures unchangingly bloom,
And our guide is the glory that shines through the tomb,
  From the ever-green mountains of life.

THE WORLD WOULD BE BETTER FOR IT.

Music by J. G. Clark.

If men cared less for wealth and fame,
  And less for battle-fields and glory;
If writ in human hearts a name
  Seemed better than in song or story;
If men, instead of nursing pride,
  Would learn to hate it and abhor it;
    If more relied
    On love to guide,
The world would be the better for it.

If men dealt less in stocks and lands,
  And more in bonds and deeds fraternal;
If love's work had more willing hands
  To link this world to the supernal;
If men stored up love's oil and wine,
  And on bruised human hearts would pour it;
    If "yours" and "mine"
    Would once combine,
The world would be the better for it.

If more would *act* the play of life,
  And fewer spoil it in rehearsal;
If bigotry would sheathe its knife
  Till good became more universal;

If custom, gray with ages grown,
  Had fewer blind men to adore it;
    If talent shone
    In truth alone,
The world would be the better for it.

If men were wise in little things,
  Affecting less in all their dealings;
If hearts had fewer rusty strings
  To isolate their kindly feelings;
If men, when wrong beats down the right,
  Would strike together and restore it;
    If right made might
    In every fight,
The world would be the better for it.

WE SHALL KNOW.

When the mists have rolled in splendor
  From the beauty of the hills,
And the sunshine, warm and tender,
  Falls in kisses on the rills,
We may read love's shining letter
  In the rainbow of the spray;
We shall know each other better
  When the mists have cleared away.

Chorus.

We shall know as we are known,
  Never more to walk alone,
In the dawning of the morning,
  When the mists have cleared away.

If we err in human blindness,
  And forget that we are dust;
If we miss the law of kindness
  When we struggle to be just;

SPIRITUAL HARMONIES.

Snowy wings of peace shall cover
　All the plain that hides away,
When the weary watch is over,
　And the mists have cleared away.
　　　　CHORUS.

When the mists have risen above us,
　As our Father knows his own,
Face to face with those that love us,
　We shall know as we are known.
Love beyond the orient meadows
　Floats the golden fringe of day;
Heart to heart, we bide the shadows
　Till the mists have cleared away.
　　　　CHORUS.

SPIRIT-LIFE REAL.

C. M.

COME, let us join our cheerful songs
　With angels round the throne;
Ten thousand thousand are their tongues,
　But all their joys are one.

O the transporting, rapt'rous scene
　That rises to my sight!
Sweet fields arrayed in living green,
　And rivers of delight!

There gen'rous fruits that never fail
　On trees immortal grow;
There rocks, and hills, and brooks, and vale,
　With milk and honey flow.

Filled with delight, my raptured soul
　Would here no longer stay;
Though Jordan's waves around me roll,
　Fearless I'd launch away.

THE LOVED NEAR US.

8's & 7's. *Leach.*

They are waiting for our coming
  On the bright celestial shore,
Where the spirit knows no sorrow,
  And the cares of life are o'er;
Where no cloud shall hide the sunlight,
  Where no tear shall dim the eye,
Where no heart shall throb with anguish,
  And the loved ones never die.

Where the springs of life eternal
  Form the silvery crystal stream,
And the seasons, ever vernal,
  Clothe the fields in living green;
Where the roses never wither,
  And the lilies never fade;
Where the brooklets murmur ever
  'Neath the forest's cooling shade.

They are ever, ever near us;
  We are never left alone;
In our daily toils they cheer us,
  And they bless our peaceful home;
Earth's short voyage will soon be over,
  Heaven's pure joys are near at hand;
Angel loved ones round us hover,
  Guiding to the "Summer Land."

FREELY GIVE.

S. M. *Lisbon — P. of L*

Go forth among the poor,
  Thy pathway leadeth there;
Thy gentle voice may soothe their pain,
  And blunt the thorns of care.

Go forth with earnest zeal,
  Nor from the duty start;
Speak to them words of gracious love, —
  Blest are the pure in heart.

Go forth through all the earth,
  There waiteth work for you;
The harvest truly seems most fair,
  But laborers are few.

With tireless, hopeful love
  Fulfil your lofty part,
And yours shall be the blessing too, —
  Blest are the pure in heart.

GLAD TIDINGS.

S. M.

How beauteous are their feet
  Who stand on Zion's hill!
Who bring salvation on their tongues,
  And words of peace reveal.

How happy are our ears
  That hear this joyful sound,
Which kings and prophets waited for,
  And sought, but never found!

How blessed are our eyes
  That see this heavenly light!
Prophets and kings desired it long,
  But died without the sight.

The watchmen join their voice,
  And tuneful notes employ:
Jerusalem breaks forth in songs,
  And deserts learn the joy.

REST.

S. M.   *St. Thomas.*

OH. where shall rest be found,
  Rest for the weary soul?
'Twere vain the ocean depths to sound,
  Or pierce to either pole.

The world can never give
  The bliss for which we sigh;
'Tis not the whole of life to live,
  Nor all of death to die.

Beyond this vale of tears
  There is a life above,
Unmeasured by the flight of years,
  And all that life is love.

HO! MY COMRADES.

P. P. Bliss.

Ho! my comrades, see the signal
  Waving in the sky!
Reinforcements now appearing,
  Victory is nigh!
CHORUS.
"Hold the fort, for I am coming,"
  Jesus signals still;
Wave the answer back to heaven —
  "By Thy grace we will."

See the mighty host advancing,
  Satan leading on;
Mighty men around us falling,
  Courage almost gone.
CHORUS.

See the glorious banner waving,
  Hear the bugle blow;
In our Leader's name we'll triumph
  Over every foe.
    CHORUS.

Fierce and long the battle rages,
  But our help is near;
Onward comes our Great Commander;
  Cheer, my comrades, cheer!
    CHORUS.

WORK, FOR THE NIGHT IS COMING.

7's & 6's, F.

Work, for the night is coming;
  Work through the morning hours;
Work while the dew is sparkling;
  Work 'mid springing flowers;
Work when the day grows brighter;
  Work in the glowing sun;
Work, for the night is coming,
  When man's work is done.

Work, for the night is coming;
  Work through the sunny noon;
Fill brightest hours with labor;
  Rest comes sure and soon.
Give every flying minute
  Something to keep in store;
Work, for the night is coming,
  When man works no more.

Work, for the night is coming,
  Under the sunset skies;
While their bright tints are glowing;
  Work, for daylight flies.

Work till the last beam fadeth,
  Fadeth to shine no more;
Work while the night is dark'ning,
  When man's work is o'er.

GONE TO DWELL WITH ANGELS.

8's & 7's.   *Page* 126, *P. of L.*

One sweet flower has drooped and faded;
  One sweet tender voice has fled;
One fair brow the grave has shaded;
  One dear schoolmate upward led.

But we feel no thought of sadness,
  For our child is happy now;
He has knelt, in soul-felt gladness,
  Where the blessed angels bow.

He has gone to heaven before us;
  But he turns and waves his hand,
Pointing to the glories o'er us,
  In that happy spirit-land.

May our footsteps never falter
  In the path that he has trod;
May we worship at the altar
  Of the great and living God.

WE'VE A HOME OVER THERE.

Oh, think of a home over there,
  By the side of the river of light!
Where the saints, all immortal and fair,
  Are robed in their garments of white.
    Over there, over there,
  Oh, think of a home over there!

Oh, think of the friends over there,
  Who before us the journey have trod!
Of the songs that they breathe on the air,
  In their home in the palace of God!
    Over there, over there,
  Oh, think of the friends over there!

I'll soon be at home over there,
  For the end of my journey I see;
Many dear to my heart over there
  Are watching and waiting for me.
    Over there, over there,
  I'll soon be at home over there.

WE SHALL BE KNOWN ABOVE.

Music by J. G. Clark.

UNDER the ice the waters run;
  Under the ice our spirits lie;
The genial glow of the summer sun
  Will loosen their fetters by and by.
    Moan and groan in your prison cold,
      River of life, river of love;
    The nights grow short, the days grow long,
    Weaker and weaker the bonds of wrong,
      And the sun shines bright above.

Under the ice, under the snow,
  Our lives are bound in a crystal ring;
By and by will the south winds blow,
  And roses bloom on the banks of spring.
    Moan and groan, etc.

Under the ice our souls are hid;
  Under the ice our good deeds grow;
Men but credit the wrong we did,
  Never the motives that lie below.
    Moan and groan, etc.

Under the ice we hide our wrong —
Under the ice that has chilled us through;
Oh, that the friends who have known us long,
Dare to doubt we are good and true!
Moan and groan, etc.

ANOTHER HAND IS BECKONING US.

C. M.   Page 59, P. of L.

Another hand is beckoning us,
Another call is given;
And glows once more with angel steps
The path that leads to heaven.

Oh, half we deemed she needed not
The changing of her sphere,
To give to heaven a shining one,
Who walked an angel here.

Unto our Father's will alone
One thought has reconciled:
That He whose love exceedeth ours
Hath taken home his child.

Fold her, O Father! in thine arms,
And let her henceforth be
A messenger of love between
Our human hearts and thee.

WAITING BY THE RIVER.

8's & 7's, C.

We are waiting by the river,
We are watching on the shore,
Only waiting for the boatman;
Soon he'll come to bear us o'er.

Though the mist hang o'er the river,
  And its billows loudly roar,
Yet we hear the song of angels,
  Wafted from the other shore.

And the bright celestial city,
  We have caught such radiant gleams
Of its towers like dazzling sunlight,
  With its sweet and peaceful streams.

When we've passed the vale of shadows,
  With its dark and chilling tide,
In that bright and glorious city
  We shall evermore abide.

SYMPATHY WITH THE AFFLICTED.

C. M.   *Page* 98, *P. of L.*

BLEST is the man whose generous heart
  Feels all another's pain,
To whom the supplicating eye
  Is never raised in vain;

Whose breast expands with generous warmth,
  A brother's woes to feel,
And bleeds in pity o'er the wound
  He wants the power to heal.

He spreads his kind, supporting arms
  To every child of grief;
His secret bounty largely flows,
  And brings unasked relief.

To gentle offices of love
  His feet are never slow;
He views, through mercy's melting eye,
  A brother in a foe.

A THANKSGIVING.

    8's & 6's, D. *Page* 200, *P. of L.*

For the wealth of pathless forests,
 Whereon no axe may fall;
For the winds that haunt the branches,
 The birdling's timid call;
For the red leaves dropped like rubies
 Upon the dark green sod;
For the waving of the forests,
 We thank thee, O our God!

For the sound of waters gushing
 In bubbling beads of light;
For the fleets of snow-white lilies,—
 Firm anchors out of sight;
For the reeds among the eddies,
 The crystal on the clod;
For the flowing of the rivers,
 We thank thee, O our God!

For the buds that throng to gladden
 The toiler's plodding way;
For the bursting of fresh roses
 With every new-born day;
For the bare twigs, that in summer
 Bloom like the prophet's rod;
For the blossoming of flowers,
 We thank thee, O our God!

NATURE A TEMPLE OF WORSHIP.

    L. M. *Page* 16, *P. of L.*

The turf shall be my fragrant shrine;
My temple, Lord, that arch of thine;
My censer's breath the mountain airs,
And silent thoughts my only prayers.

My choir shall be the moonlight waves,
When murmuring homeward to their caves,
Or when the stillness of the sea,
Even more than music, breathes of Thee.

I'll seek, by day, some glade unknown,
All light and silence, like thy throne;
And the pale stars shall be, at night,
The only eyes that watch my rite.

Thy heaven, on which 'tis bliss to look,
Shall be my pure and shining book,
Where I shall read, in words of flame,
The glories of thy wondrous name.

A LIGHT IN THE WINDOW.

There's a light in the window for thee, brother;
  There's a light in the window for thee.
A dear one has passed to the mansion above;
  There's a light in the window for thee.

Chorus.
A mansion in heaven we see,
  And a light in the window for thee;
A mansion in heaven we see,
  And a light in the window for thee.

There's a crown, and a robe, and a palm, brother,
  When from toil and from care you are free;
While angel friends there who have gone to prepare
  A light in the window for thee.
Chorus.

Oh, watch, and be faithful, and hope, brother,
  All your journey o'er life's troubled sea;
Though afflictions assail you, and storms beat severe,
  There's a light in the window for thee.
Chorus.

ANGEL CARE.

Soft and low those angel voices
 Come to breathe in love a prayer,
And the weary heart rejoices
 In sweet thoughts of angel care.

Chorus.

Going with us, caring for us,
 As life's journey we pursue;
Going with us, caring for us,
 Till our distant homes we view.

Come to breathe on us a blessing,
 As in harmony we meet,
And with friendly hands caressing
 Us as we their presence greet.
Chorus.

Come to make our burdens lighter
 By their teaching how to live;
Teachings purer, better, brighter,
 Than our earthly friends can give.
Chorus.

Come to lead us on forever
 Up progression's shining road
Where the soul shall weary never,
 'Midst the wondrous works of God.
Chorus.

THERE'S A LAND OF FADELESS BEAUTY.

There's a land of fadeless beauty,
 Bright beyond the narrow sea,
Where the rainbow lasts forever,
 And the stars eternal be;

Homes no human hands can fashion
  There forever shall endure;
Spirits free from earthly passion,
  Deathless spirits glad and pure.

There's a land whose chilly winter
  Never spreads its frosty gloom;
Where no deadly blight can wither
  Gardens of perennial bloom.
'Tis a land where never sorrow
  Bids the mourner's tear to flow;
Where no frowning dark to-morrow
  Ever dawns on human woe.

Yet in all my finest fancy
  Never rose so fair a dream
As this land beyond the waters
  Doth to eyes celestial seem:
Where, in love's embraces folden,
  I my cherished friends shall see:
Oh, this clime so glorious, golden,
  Holds a happy home for me!

EVENING.

8's & 7's, 6 Lines.
Page 31, *S. H.*

GENTLE twilight, softly stealing
  O'er the busy scenes of earth,
Brings a beautiful revealing
  Of the spirit's holier worth, —
    Sweet revealing
  Of the spirit's holier worth.

Filled with meditative musing,
  Sits the calm, communing soul;
Stars of twilight soft diffusing
  Evening incense as they roll.
    Soft diffusing
  Evening incense as they roll.

Brightest of the orbs there beaming,
  Heavenly lamps hung out above,
Shines the lamp of truth redeeming,
  Star of God's unfailing love, —
    Truth redeeming,
  Star of God's unfailing love.

Holy star, so mildly shining,
  With thy pure, celestial ray,
Let my heart, its love entwining,
  Feel the dawn of heavenly day, —
    Love entwining,
  Feel the dawn of heavenly day.

WHAT SHALL THE HARVEST BE?

"Whatsoever a man soweth, that shall he also reap."
GAL. vi. 7.

Page 76, G. H.

Sowing the seed by the daylight fair,
Sowing the seed by the noonday glare,
Sowing the seed by the fading light.
Sowing the seed in the solemn night, —
  Oh, what shall the harvest be?
  Oh, what shall the harvest be?

CHORUS.

Sown in the darkness or sown in the light,
Sown in our weakness or sown in our might,
Gathered in time or eternity,
  Sure, ah, sure will the harvest be!

Sowing the seed by the wayside high,
Sowing the seed on the rocks to die,
Sowing the seed where the thorns will spoil,
Sowing the seed in the fertile soil, —
  Oh, what shall the harvest be?
    CHORUS.

Sowing the seed of a lingering pain,
Sowing the seed of a maddened brain,
Sowing the seed of a tarnished name,
Sowing the seed of sorrowing shame, —
  Oh, what shall the harvest be?
        CHORUS.

Sowing the seed with an aching heart,
Sowing the seed while the tear-drops start,
Sowing in hope till the reapers come,
Gladly to gather the harvest home, —
  Oh, what shall the harvest be?
        CHORUS.

YIELD NOT TO TEMPTATION.

Music, page 87, *G. H. & S. S. No.* 1

YIELD not to temptation,
  For yielding is sin;
Each victory will help you
  Some other to win;
Fight manfully onward,
  Dark passions subdue,
Look ever to Jesus,
  He'll carry you through.

      CHORUS.
Ask the Saviour to help you,
Comfort, strengthen, and keep you;
He is willing to aid you;
  He will carry you through.

Shun evil companions,
  Bad language disdain;
God's name hold in rev'rence,
  Nor take it in vain.

Be thoughtful and earnest,
  Kind-hearted and true;
Look ever to Jesus,
  He'll carry you through.
    CHORUS.

To him that o'ercometh
  God giveth a crown:
Through faith we shall conquer,
  Though often cast down;
He who is a Saviour
  Our strength will renew;
Look ever to Jesus,
  He'll carry you through.
    CHORUS.

THE ANGEL GUEST.

L. M.   *Page* 53, *P. of L*

WITH what divine affections bold,
  How pure in heart and sound in head,
Should be the man whose thought would hold
  An hour's communion with the dead.

Oh, not the harsh and scornful word
  The victory over wrong can gain;
Not the dark prison, nor the sword,
  The shackle, or the weary chain.

But from our spirit there must flow
  A love that will the wrong outweigh;
Our lips must only blessings know,
  And wrath and sin shall die away.

'Twas Heaven that formed the holy plan
  To lead the wanderer home by love;
Thus let us save our brother man,
  And imitate our God above.

OUR BROTHER MAN.

11's & 10's.   *Whittier.*

OH, brother man, fold to thy heart thy brother!
  Where pity dwells, a heavenly peace is there;
To worship rightly is to love each other;
  Each smile a hymn, each kindly deed a prayer.

Follow with reverent steps each great example
  Of all whose holy work was doing good;
So shall the wide earth seem a sacred temple,
  Each loving life a psalm of gratitude.

Then shall all shackles fall; the stormy clangor
  Of wild war-music o'er the world shall cease;
Love shall tread out the baleful fire of anger,
  And in its ashes plant the tree of peace.

I NEED THEE EVERY HOUR.

Page 5, G. H.

I NEED Thee every hour;
  Most gracious Lord;
No tender voice like thine
  Can peace afford.

CHORUS.

I need Thee! Oh, I need Thee!
  Every hour I need Thee!
Oh, bless me now, my Father!
  I come to Thee!

I need Thee every hour;
  Let angels come
And make me thine indeed,
  Thy will be done.

CHORUS.

I need Thee every hour,
  Stay Thou near by;
Temptations lose their power
  When Thou art nigh.
    CHORUS.

I need Thee every hour,
  In joy or pain;
Come quickly and abide,
  Or life is vain.
    CHORUS.

I need Thee every hour,
  Teach me thy will;
And thy rich promises
  In me fulfil.
    CHORUS.

DEATH.

C. M.   *Page 66, P. of L.*

DEATH is the mightier second birth,
  The unveiling of the soul;
'Tis freedom from the chains of earth,
  The pilgrim's heavenly goal.

Death is the close of life's alarms,
  The watch-light on the shore;
The clasping in immortal arms
  Of loved ones gone before.

Death is a song from seraph lips,
  The day-spring from on high;
The ending of the soul's eclipse, —
  Its transit to the sky.

CROWN OF THORNS.

S. M.   *Page* 77, *S. H.*

Beside the toilsome way,
  'Mid fruits and flowers unblest,
My feet tread sadly day by day,
  Longing in vain for rest.

Ever an angel walks,
  With eyes cast meekly down,
While from the leaves and withered stalks
  She weaves my fitting crown.

What sweet and patient grace,
  E'er beaming true and kind,
Of suffering borne, rests on her face,
  So pure, so glorified!

Angel, behold, I wait,
  Crowned for life's weary hours:
Wait till thy hand shall ope the gate,
  And change the thorns to flowers.

THE GATE AJAR FOR ME.

There is a gate that stands ajar,
  And through its portals gleaming
A radiance from the cross afar,
  The Saviour's love revealing.

Chorus.
  Oh, angel friends, and can it be
  That gate was left ajar for me?
    For you, for me, —
    Was left ajar for me?

That gate ajar stands free for all
  Who seek through it salvation, —

The rich, the poor, the great and small,
  Of every tribe and nation.
      CHORUS.

Press onward, then, though foes may frown,
  For heaven's gate is open;
Accept the truth, and win the crown,
  Love's everlasting token.
      CHORUS.

Beyond the river's brink we see
  The friends that here were given;
They wear the crown of life to-day,
  They love us still in heaven.
      CHORUS.

ANGEL MOTHER.

8's & 7's.

Page 28, Spirit Minstrel

ANGEL-MOTHER, long I listened,
  Listened with attentive ear,
And my eyes with tear-drops glistened
  When I knew that thou wast near;
Thou, my guardian spirit ever,
  Ever through this lower sphere,
Till the hand of death shall sever
  Every tie that binds me here.

Angel-mother, life is dearer,
  Dearer since my doubts are flown,
And the lamp of life burns clearer
  When the way of truth is known.
Joys serene are stealing o'er me,
  O'er me joys before unknown:
Lights celestial beam before me,
  Flowers are on my pathway strewn.

THE PSALM OF LIFE.

   8's & 7's.   *Longfellow*

TELL me not in mournful numbers
 Life is but an empty dream;
For the soul is dead that slumbers,
 And things are not what they seem.

In the world's broad field of battle,
 In the bivouac of life,
Be not like dumb, driven cattle!
 Be a hero in the strife!

Lives of great men all remind us
 We can make our lives sublime,
And, departing, leave behind us
 Footsteps on the sands of time —

Footsteps that, perhaps, another,
 Sailing o'er life's solemn main,
A forlorn and shipwrecked brother,
 Seeing, shall take heart again.

Let us, then, be up and doing,
 With a heart for any fate;
Still achieving, still pursuing,
 Learn to labor and to wait.

PROGRESS.

   8's, 3's, & 7's.

MEN of thought, be up and stirring,
 Night and day;
Sow the seed, withdraw the curtain,
 Clear the way!
Men of action, aid and cheer them
 As ye may;

There's a fount about to stream;
There's a light about to beam;
There's a warmth about to glow;
There's a flower about to blow;
There's a midnight blackness changing
    Into gray.
Men of thought and men of action,
    Clear the way.

Once the welcome light has broken,
    Who shall say
What the unimagined glories
    Of the day?
What the evil that shall perish
    In its ray?
Aid the dawning, tongue and pen;
Aid it, hopes of honest men;
Aid it, paper; aid it, type;
Aid it, for the hour is ripe;
And our earnest must not slacken
    Into play.
Men of thought and men of action,
    Clear the way!

COMFORTING WORDS,

FOR FUNERALS.

The Lord is my shepherd; I shall not want.
He maketh me to lie down in green pastures; he leadeth me beside the still waters. He restoreth my soul.
Yea, though I walk through the valley of the shadow of death, I will fear no evil: for thou art with me; thy rod and thy staff they comfort me.
For we know that if our earthly house of this tabernacle were dissolved, we have a building of God, a house not made with hands, eternal in the heavens.
The things which are seen are temporal; but the things which are not seen are eternal.
And as we have borne the image of the earthy, we shall also bear the image of the heavenly.
For now we see through a glass, darkly; but then face to face: now I know in part; but then shall I know even as also I am known.
For this corruptible must put on incorruption, and this mortal must put on immortality.
So when this corruptible shall have put on incorruption, and this mortal shall have put on immortality, then shall be brought to pass the saying that is written, Death is swallowed up in victory.
O death, where is thy sting? O grave, where is thy victory?

> There is a land mine eye hath seen
> In visions of enraptured thought,
> So bright that all which spreads between
> Is with its radiant glory fraught;

> A land upon whose blissful shore
> There rests no shadow, falls no stain;
> There those who meet shall part no more,
> And those long parted meet again.

Life and death are but tremulous ripples upon the placid ocean of existence; and each in its turn and time is equally beautiful. The world of spirits is real and substantial. We know our friends — know as we are known in spirit-life.

As fragrance flows from blossoms, so spiritual elements constantly rise from the material world. The refined spiritual essences from this and other planetary worlds ascending into those vast ether regions, condense and gravitate, like purpling clouds fringed with gold, to their appropriate positions. These silver-edged strata, as arching zones stretching along the measureless blue above us, are not only too magnificent for description, but they are the homes of our loved ones in heaven.

The spiritual world, all bathed in the magnetic sunlight of an eternal morning, is no shadowy realm, but real and permanent, — "a city that hath foundation, whose maker and builder is God." There are forests, fields, mountains, valleys, groves, gardens, fruits, flowers, sparkling fountains, flowing rivers, pleasant grottos; palatial mansions with gorgeous domes, constellated and astral; cottages and princely palaces with tessellated floors, tapestried walls, diamond-pointed ceilings, and scenery of transcendent loveliness. Over the portals of each holy habitation is inscribed Purity. Spirits residing within these angelic homes begin to fathom the riches of true love — *love* such as glowed in the soul of John when he leaned upon the tender bosom of Jesus.

The children of earth peopling the heavenly abodes of the hereafter, having passed through the disciplines of earth and the schoolings pertaining to the spirit-spheres, are earnest and untiring in their spiritual activities. Remembering their lives on earth, deep and holy are their sympathies for humanity. Love never forgets. In the morning-time and the gray of evening, down golden-tided rivers sail these ministering spirits of God to catch the incense of each soul-felt prayer. They come to impress and inspire. Their magnetisms are baptisms, their words the spirit-echoes of eternal life.

None say, in the summer-land of spirit-life, "I tread the wine-press alone." The law of harmonial associations is there fully realized. Those receptions of infants by matronly bands; those schools of tenderest discipline; those homes of mutual love embowered in roses; those palaces of art tinged with electric light; those cities of scientists, brotherhoods of philanthropists, and congresses of angels, — *all* add to the beatific glories of life in the republics of heaven. Those gifted with open vision, catching glimpses of landscapes and surpassingly beautiful scenery, often listen to the converse and the musical words of the immortals.

> There is a world that few have seen,
>   That wasting time can ne'er destroy,
> Where mortal footstep hath not been,
>   Nor ear hath caught its sounds of joy.
>
> It is all holy and serene, —
>   The land of glory and repose;
> And there, to dim the radiant scene,
>   No tear of sorrow ever flows.
>
> It is not fanned by summer gale;
>   'Tis not refreshed by vernal showers;
> It never needs the moonbeam pale,
>   For there are known no evening hours.
>
> There forms unseen by mortal eye,
>   Too glorious for our sight to bear,
> Are walking with their God on high,
>   And waiting our arrival there.

APPROPRIATE FOR LITTLE CHILDREN.

Infants are emblems of innocence, and little children may be compared to vines and olive-branches growing up in our homes. The angels love these buds — these little ones whose feet make music around our firesides; and when, from sickness or death, they fade from earth, they are transplanted into heaven, where loving mothers and holy angels become their teachers.

In Rama was there a voice heard, lamentation, and weeping, and great mourning, Rachel weeping for her children, and would not be comforted, because they are not.

Children are a heritage of the Lord:

They shall be mine, saith the Lord of hosts, in that day when I make up my jewels.

Our sons shall be as plants grown up in their youth; and our daughters as corner-stones, polished after the similitude of a palace:

The promise is unto you, and to your children, and to all that are afar off.

And when the child was grown, it fell on a day that he went out to his father to the reapers.

And he said unto his father, My head, my head. And he said to a lad, Carry him to his mother.

And when he had taken him, and brought him to his mother, he sat on her knees till noon, and then died.

And they brought young children unto Jesus, that he should touch them; and his disciples rebuked those who brought them.

But when Jesus saw it, he was much displeased, and said unto them, Suffer the little children to come unto me, and forbid them not: for of such is the kingdom of God.

Verily I say unto you, Whosoever shall not receive the kingdom of God as a little child, he shall not enter therein.

And he took them up in his arms, put his hands upon them, and blessed them.

And he saith unto them, Take heed that ye despise not one of these little ones: for I say unto you, That in heaven their angels do always behold the face of my Father which is in heaven.

> Childish feet are straying homeward,
>   Some have entered there to-day,
> Passed, perchance, from paths of darkness,
>   To the peace for which we pray;
> Gone we know not from what suffering,
>   Fled we know not from what sin;
> O ye gates that open heavenward,
>   Swing together, shut them in!
>
> They at least are safe from falling
>   On the battlefield of life,
> Overcome, as thousands have been,
>   By temptation, care, and strife;
> And have died with hands close gathered
>   In the tender clasp of ours;
> God be thanked that we could fold them
>   Pure as snow and full of flowers!
>
> So, O angels, to your keeping
>   Give we what we call "our own,"
> Gone a little time before us
>   Through the portals leading Home;
> They are safe from pain and sorrow,
>   We alone can bear the rod,
> With these blossoms safely nurtured
>   In the garden of our God.

APPROPRIATE FOR PARENTS AND FOR THE AGED.

As for man, his days are as grass; as a flower of the field, so he flourisheth.

For the wind passeth over it, and it is gone; and the place thereof shall know it no more.

Thou hast made us, and not we ourselves. We are thy people, and the sheep of thy pasture.

Furthermore, we have had fathers of our flesh which corrected us, and we gave them reverence: shall we not much rather be in subjection unto the Father of spirits, and live?

For they verily for a few days chastened us after their own pleasure; but he for our profit, that we might be partakers of his holiness.

Now no chastening for the present seemeth to be joyous, but grievous: nevertheless, afterward it yieldeth the peaceable fruit of righteousness unto them which are exercised thereby.

Mark the perfect man, and behold the upright: for the end of that man is peace.

Let me die the death of the righteous, and let my last end be like his!

Know ye not that there is a prince and a great man fallen this day in Israel?

All ye that are about him, bemoan him; and all ye that know his name, say, How is the strong staff broken, and the beautiful rod!

None of us liveth to himself, and no man dieth to himself.

For whether we live, we live unto the Lord; and whether we die, we die unto the Lord: whether we live, therefore, or die, we are the Lord's.

Though he take away the strong man from among us, yet will he not forsake us in our trouble.

Though we be bowed down with mourning, yet hath the Lord been gracious unto us and blessed us.

The memory of the just is blessed:

I have seen the good man in power, and my heart was glad within me.

He was eyes to the blind, and feet was he to the lame.

He was a father to the poor; and the cause which he knew not he searched out.

Unto him men gave ear, and waited and kept silence at his counsel.

The days of our years are threescore years and ten;

and if by reason of strength they be fourscore years, yet is their strength labor and sorrow; for it is soon cut off, and we fly away.

So teach us to number our days, that we may apply our hearts unto wisdom.

They go down to the grave in a full age, like as a shock of corn cometh in his season.

The glory of young men is their strength: and the beauty of old men is the gray head.

The hoary head is a crown of glory, if it be found in the way of righteousness.

I am now ready to be offered, and the time of my departure is at hand.

I have fought a good fight, I have finished my course, I have kept the faith:

Henceforth there is laid up for me a crown of righteousness, which the Lord, the righteous Judge, shall give me at that day.

A MOTHER.

He that honoreth his mother is as one that layeth up treasure.

For who is like a mother among all them that are in the earth.

She openeth her mouth with wisdom; and in her tongue is the law of kindness.

She looketh well to the ways of her household, and eateth not the bread of idleness.

Her children arise up, and call her blessed; her husband also, and he praiseth her.

Precious shall be her memory when she goeth down to the grave, and the remembrance of her goodness shall be as a healing balm.

Lord, thou hast been our dwelling-place in all generations. Before the mountains were brought forth, or ever thou hadst formed the earth and the world, even from everlasting to everlasting, thou art God.

The Lord is good to all: and his tender mercies are over all his works.

Then shall the dust return to the earth as it was: and the spirit shall return unto God who gave it.

And God shall wipe away all tears from their eyes; and there shall be no more death, neither sorrow, nor crying, neither shall there be any more pain: for the former things are passed away.

Who are these which are arrayed in white robes? and whence came they?

And I said unto him, Sir, thou knowest. And he said to me, These are they which came out of great tribulation, and have washed their robes, and made them white.

Let not your heart be troubled: ye believe in God, believe also in me.

In my Father's house are many mansions: if it were not so, I would have told you. I go to prepare a place for you.

And if I go and prepare a place for you, I will come again and receive you unto myself; that where I am, there ye may be also.

Why mourn ye that our aged friend is dead?
Ye are not sad to see the gathered grain,
Nor when their mellow fruit the orchards cast,
Nor when the yellow woods shake down the ripened
    mast.

Ye sigh not when the sun, his course fulfilled,
    His glorious course, rejoicing earth and sky,
In the soft evening, when the winds are stilled,
    Sinks where his islands of refreshment lie,

Her youth was innocent; her riper age
    Marked with some act of goodness every day;
And watched by eyes that loved her, calm and sage,
    Faded her late declining years away.
Cheerful she gave her being up, and went
To share the holy rest that waits a life well spent.

GENERAL INDEX.

Spiritualism, and its General Teachings.

	PAGE
What is Spiritualism?	5
Readings and Responses	8
Progress and the Victory	16

Spiritual Hymns and Songs.

The Evergreen Shore	18
Let the Good Angels come in	19
Oh, sing to me of Heaven	20
A New Religion	20
Come, Gentle Spirits	21
The Shining Shore	22
The Beautiful River	22
The Morning Light	23
Joy to the World	24
Nearer, my God, to Thee	25
Are we not Brothers all?	25
The Entertaining Sight	26
How Cheering the Thought	27
Welcome, Angels	27
The Tie of Brotherhood	28
The Eden Above	28
Sweet By-and-by	29
Bright Hills of Glory	30
Home, Sweet Home	30
Protecting Power	31
Rest for the Weary	32

GENERAL INDEX.

The Beautiful Land	33
Our Loved in Heaven	34
There is Joy for You	35
Hand in Hand with Angels	35
The Beautiful	36
Sherburne	37
Dreaming To-night	38
Exaltation	39
The Bower of Prayer	39
I'm a Pilgrim	40
Shall we know each other there?	41
The Bright Land of Beulah	42
Sweet Hour of Prayer	43
The Eden of Love	43
The Pilgrim Stranger	44
When shall we meet again?	45
America	46
We love the Father	47
The Missionary Hymn	47
Footsteps of Angels	48
Voices from the Spirit-Land	49
Angel Friends	50
My Angel Name	51
Celestial Greetings	52
The Deeds of Charity	52
Prayer	53
Home of the Soul	54
Darling Nelly Gray	54
Lord, dismiss us	55
Equality	56
When shall we all meet again?	57
God is forever with Man	57
Pilgrim's Happy Lot	58
Where the Roses ne'er shall wither	59
I'm Happy	60
Royal Proclamation	61
The Sweet Story	61
There's a Land far away	62
The World would be better for it	63
We shall know	64
Spirit-Life real	66

GENERAL INDEX.

The Loved near us 66
Freely give 66
Glad Tidings 67
Rest 68
Ho! my Comrades 68
Work, for the Night is coming . . . 69
Gone to dwell with Angels 70
We've a Home over there 70
We shall be known Above 71
Another Hand is beckoning us . . . 72
Waiting by the River 72
Sympathy with the Afflicted 73
A Thanksgiving 74
Nature a Temple of Worship 74
A Light in the Window 75
Angel Care 76
Evening 77
What shall the Harvest be? 78
Yield not to Temptation 79
The Angel Guest 80
Our Brother Man 81
I need Thee every Hour 81
Death 82
Crown of Thorns 83
The Gate ajar for me 83
Angel Mother 84
The Psalm of Life 85
Progress 85

COMFORTING WORDS, FOR FUNERALS . . 87

APPROPRIATE FOR LITTLE CHILDREN . . 90

APPROPRIATE FOR PARENTS AND FOR THE AGED. 91

A MOTHER 93

INDEX OF FIRST LINES

OF

SPIRITUAL HYMNS AND SONGS.

	PAGE
A beautiful land of joy I see	33
All men are equal in their birth	56
A new religion shakes the earth	20
Angel-mother, long I listened	84
Another hand is beckoning us	72
Beside the toilsome way	83
Blest be the tie that binds	28
Blest is the man whose generous heart	73
Come, all ye loved, to wisdom's mountain	34
Come, gentle spirits, to us now	21
Come, let us join our cheerful songs	65
Death is the mightier second birth	82
Floating on the breath of evening	50
For the wealth of pathless forests	74
From Greenland's icy mountains	47
Go forth among the poor	66
Gentle twilight, softly stealing	77
Hand in hand with angels	35
Hear the royal proclamation	61
Heirs of the morning, we walk in the light	57
Ho! my comrades, see the signal	68
How beauteous are their feet	67
How cheering the thought, that the angels of God	27
How sweet to reflect on the joys that await me	43
Hushed be the battle's fearful roar	25
If men cared less for wealth and fame	63
I'm happy, I'm happy! O wondrous account	60

INDEX OF FIRST LINES.

I'm a pilgrim, and I'm a stranger	40
I need Thee every hour	81
In the angels' home in glory	32
In the land where I am going	51
I think, when I read that sweet story of old	61
I will sing you a song of that beautiful land	54
Joy to the world — the darkness flies	24
Lord, dismiss us with thy blessing	55
Lo! what an entertaining sight	26
Men of thought, be up and stirring	85
My country, 'tis of thee	46
My days are gliding swiftly by	22
My latest sun is sinking fast	42
Nearer, my God, to Thee	25
No foot of land do I possess	58
Oh, brother man, fold to thy heart thy brother	81
Oh, give me a harp on the bright hills of glory	30
Oh, let not your hearts be troubled	35
Oh, sing to me of heaven	20
Oh, think of a home over there	70
Oh, where shall rest be found	68
One sweet flower has drooped and faded	70
Peace be thine, the angels greet thee	52
Prayer is the soul's sincere desire	53
Shall we gather at the river	22
Soft and low those angel voices	76
Sowing the seed by the daylight fair	78
Sweet hour of prayer! sweet hour of prayer	43
Tell me not in mournful numbers	85
The man of charity extends	52
The morning light is breaking	23
The turf shall be my fragrant shrine	74
The world has much of beautiful	36
There is a gate that stands ajar	83
There's a land far away 'mid the stars, we are told	62
There's a land of fadeless beauty	76
There's a land that is fairer than day	29
There's a light in the window for thee, brother	75
There's a low, green valley on the old Kentucky shore	54
They are waiting for our coming	66

They hover around us, bright angels are near . 19
This world of strife is not our home . . 18
Though far o'er the wide earth our footsteps may
   roam 30
To leave my dear friends, and with neighbors to
   part. 39
Under the ice the waters run 71
We are waiting by the river 72
Welcome, angels pure and bright . . . 27
We love the Father, He's so good . . . 47
We're bound for the land of the pure and the holy 28
We're dreaming to-night of the loved ones dear . 38
When shall we all meet again 57
When shall we meet again 45
When the hours of day are numbered . . 48
When the mists have rolled in splendor . . 64
When we hear the music ringing . . . 41
Where is the soul's sincere desire . . . 53
Where the roses ne'er shall wither . . . 59
While shepherds watched their flocks by night . 37
While Thee I seek, protecting power . . 31
Whither goest thou, pilgrim stranger . . . 44
With what divine affections bold . . . 80
Work, for the night is coming 69
Ye realms below the skies 99
Yield not to temptation 79

www.ingramcontent.com/pod-product-compliance
Lightning Source LLC
Chambersburg PA
CBHW020859160426
43192CB00007B/995